GEL PEN
flowers

By Patricia Petrakis

Copyright © 2021 Patricia Petrakis.

All rights reserved. This book or any portion thereof may not be reproduced or used in any manner whatsoever without the express written permission of the publisher except for the use of brief quotations in a book review.

CONTENTS

Preface 1
Introduction: The Drop Off 3
Chapter 1: Gel Pen Flowers 5
    Thoughts On The Drop Off: 11
Chapter 2: Into The Foster Funnel 13
    Foster Care 15
    To The I Love You Bully 27
    Thoughts On Foster Care 29
Chapter 3: The Joys Of A Name 31
    New Name Thoughts 46
Chapter 4: The Honeymoon Stage 49
    Thoughts On The Honeymoon Stage 62
Chapter 5: How To Deal 65
    Thoughts On How To Deal 76
Chapter 6: Growing Pains 79
    The Nightmare 88
    Thoughts On Growing Pains 92
Chapter 7: Good Grief 97
    Thoughts On Good Grief 119
    The Whispers/The Ugly Truth 121
    Conclusion Part Of 'The Whispers' 132
    Interlude: A Dash Of This And A Splash Of That 135

Chapter 8: The Ongoing Ding 137
    Thoughts On The Ongoing Ding... 150
Chapter 9: Dancing With Paintbrushes 153
    Thoughts On Dancing With Paintbrushes 158
    The Not-So-Ugly Truth... 159
    Wrapping Up The Ugly Truth... 160
Chapter 10: Seasons Greetings... 161
    Thoughts On Seasons Greetings 166
Chapter 11: God Said 'Let There Be Courage'................................ 167
    Thoughts On God Said, Let There Be Courage.................... 173
Chapter 12: The Restraining Order 175
    July 2, Court Date.. 181
    Thoughts On The Restraining Order 184
Chapter 13: One Year Later 185
    Thoughts On A Year Later.. 190
Chapter 14: Relationships, Flowers, and Therapy...Oh My 191
Acknowledgments... 211

PREFACE

Hey there, I can't believe you're holding me in your hands. I feel so honored. You are one of the few people who read the prefaces to books, and that alone makes you magical and my kind of person.

Okay, onto a short disclaimer: everything in this book is based off my memories and encounters, the way I remember them. I don't lay claim to other people's stories or experiences. Gel Pen Flowers is a work of nonfiction but some names and identifying details have been changed for obvious reasons. Gel Pen Flowers covers topics such as child, sexual and mental abuse, suicidal thoughts, drug addiction, and death. Pretty much a lot of life's sadness. It is also filled with humor, celebration, and ordinary examples of extraordinary love.

Oh, crap, I lost some people... Was that too real?

On the humor point – that's just the way I deal with trauma, death, being uncomfortable and all that jazz. If you think that it's silly or evasive, that's okay. I still encourage you to read on because it's always good to hear another person's point of view even if you don't agree with it.

INTRODUCTION

THE DROP OFF

I love the rain. There is something about just standing in it for a few minutes that refreshes my soul. Plus, have you ever run in the rain while listening to Trans-Siberian Orchestra? It's blissful, the whole experience leaves me with a feeling of tranquility that is hard to describe. I highly recommend starting with 'Wizards in Winter – Instrumental' followed by 'Faith Noel'. Talk about the perfect intro to get you in the zone! Anyway, this isn't a story about my running playlist. The first time I truly felt the rain was in 1995 after walking for miles in the middle of the night barefoot. My feet felt raw and the reflection of the streetlights hurt my eyes against the pure black rainy sky. I had no idea what was going on and why we were walking, all I wanted to do was sleep. But the rain; the rain made me shiver, it kept me calm. In my state of exhausted confusion, I found some sort of comfort in feeling the drizzle against my skin. We'd been walking for what felt like hours and every time I tried to stop, I kept being pulled forward by my mom, Lynn. When we finally came to a standstill, it was at a stranger's house in the middle of nowhere and Lynn knocked on the door and then walked away. The next day I woke up hiding in the closet with my older brother Robert, covering my ears against the screams we heard from outside. Then everything went quiet and a young woman cracked the door open and told us not to make a sound and to sit still. Shortly after that, she brought us out of our hiding spot and a man from the Department of Children and Families was there to pick us up. Just like that, we entered the Foster Care System.

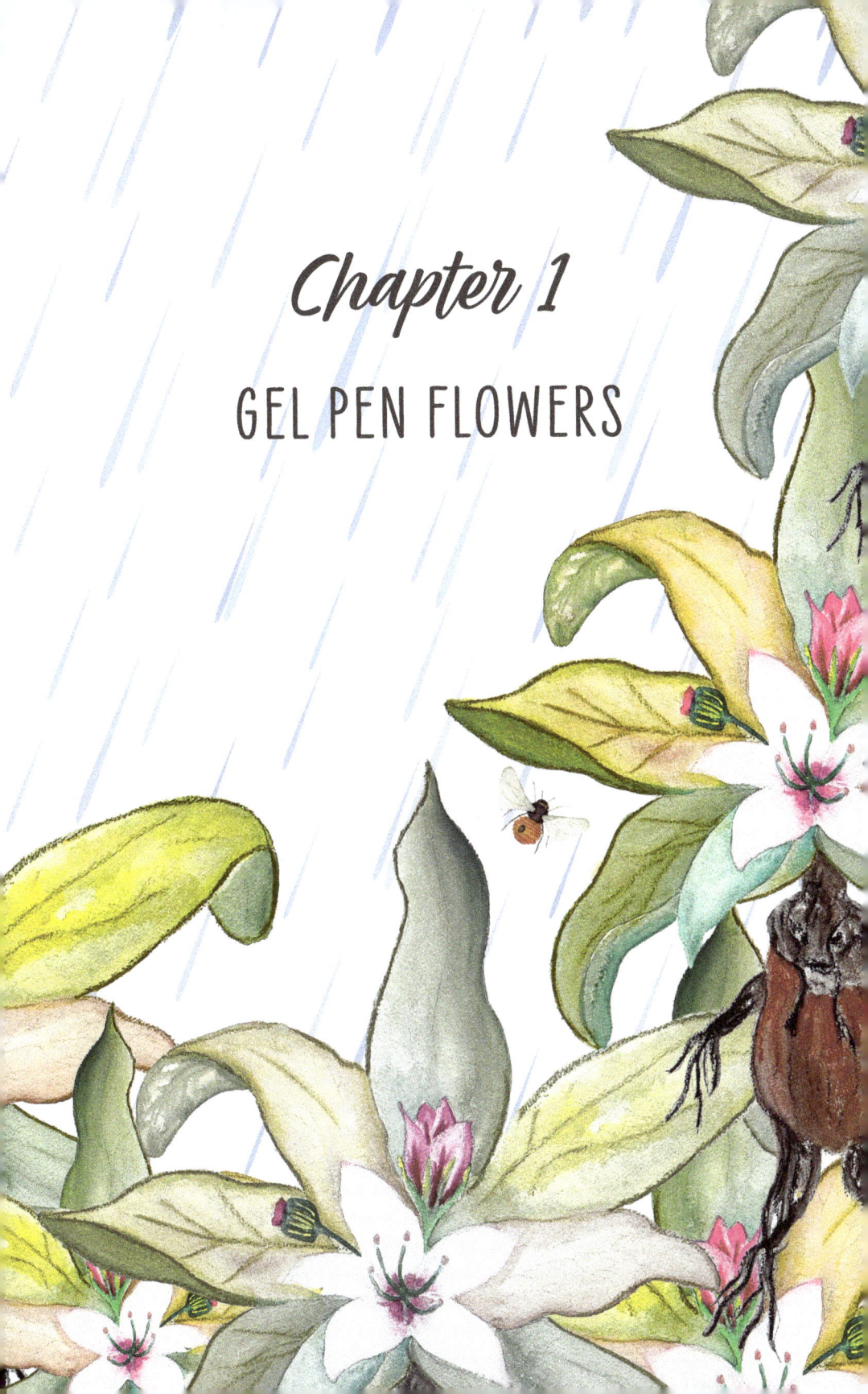

Chapter 1
GEL PEN FLOWERS

1

What came after that was an endless number of fluorescent lights, cold offices, and random people's houses. It was miserable and a blur all at the same time. I'm pretty sure my loathing for yellow fluorescent lights came from those days or weeks in and out of the DCF office building. As someone who went through the experience and now has a degree in Psychology, I'd like to offer some advice to whoever is in charge, and that is to make those offices more inviting. Especially if you're going to be bringing kids in after they were just dropped off at a random stranger's house. Office environments don't have to project the message that all is doomed and our souls have no chance! Take out the horrible lighting, add comfy furniture. Maybe throw in a warm snack and juice pack. I understand that means a budget for snacks but, come on, it's for the kids.

As much I'm complaining about the office building, the truth is DCF was a cold, ugly lit, no-snack heaven in my eyes. Before that rainy night, Robert and I were used as human punching bags for Lynn's boyfriend to release his anger on after a stressful a day. His name was Junior, he was a construction worker who came off as a family guy and the life of the party. You know that guy. When really, his outwards persona masked his true self – he was an abuser. Looking back on what he did to us makes me sick. You see, Junior was anything but a family guy, he would stab Robert in the forehead with forks for fun and put his cigarettes out on me for not understanding Spanish. He thought I was his biological daughter and was disappointed in me for not knowing his language. Whatever I got was half of what Robert got, though, because he had a different dad. Robert's dad was a truck driver who thought leaving him with our mom was best for him. In Junior's eyes that meant Robert deserved to be punished more because he wasn't his. Junior loved to play a game during naptime that involved dragging us out of bed by our hair and beating us if we weren't asleep in a certain amount of time. He'd know because he'd walk over and pull up our eye lids to see if we were asleep.

    One nap, I was playing with the sunlight on the wall and didn't hear him coming. Before I knew it, my head was yanked back; I barely touched the floor as he pulled me from the top bunk towards his bedroom. Robert jumped in and started hitting the back of Juniors legs, trying to pull me away from his grip. Frustrated, Junior threw me against the wall, turned around and started to pound Robert in the head multiple times while holding him up by his shirt. How it ended is unclear, but I later learned that Robert ended up getting punched in the head so severely that it caused permanent damage. Lynn, our mom, she was there the whole time but didn't do anything because that meant Junior would take it out on her. So instead, she would get high and pretty much disappear. When Junior wasn't home, she would dance to 'I Like It, I Love It' by Tim McGraw and we would pick flowers in the front yard. She always smelt of cigarettes and tanning oil and had the prettiest curls. She was like sunlight in those moments. That version of her was only fleeting though. She was young and a drug addict who Junior had total control over. The version of her I remember most is her having a seizure outside the neighbor's house. Our neighbor was an older lady who snuck Robert and I Honey Buns and chocolate milk when Lynn and Jr weren't watching us. I liked her and wished she was allowed to hang out with us more, but once the adults were in sight she always went back inside and shut the door. It was like she knew we weren't in good hands but couldn't do anything about it. The one time she stepped in was when Lynn was laying down in the middle of the road shaking violently as Robert and I were trying to help her since Junior had told us to leave her and walked away.

Shortly after the seizure Junior talked Lynn into giving us our own rooms. We lived in a two-bedroom house which meant Robert didn't get his own room and he was sleeping on a rug outback. I didn't know that until years later in a counseling session. His memories and mine were different but not too far apart. Together we were able to piece things together like a torn photo until the picture became clear. We discovered that what we thought was the ocean in our back yard was Lake Apopka, a gigantic lake that, to my mind, stretched far out into the horizon. I should have known it was a lake by all the trees that surrounded it and the tiny broken-down docks outside the broken-down homes around us. To me though, the lake felt safe; every time I looked out at the open water there was a feeling of vast opportunity, like I knew there was something better waiting for me, and I just had to figure out how to get it.

After discovering where Robert slept and remembering the hall to the room we shared, a fear I had of a door cracking open resurfaced for me in that session. Once Robert and I were separated Junior would visit us separately at night. The house would be quiet, and I'd hear his footsteps get louder and louder before they came to a complete stop outside my room. Then, he'd slowly crack the door until the light shined behind his figure, creating a shadow standing in the hall. Once he got me out of bed, he'd take me into the bathroom and run a bath. He would start by washing my hair and finished with sending me back to bed. He made visiting my room a weekly routine but this one time I snuck in my kitten Tigger, and it scratched him, causing Lynn to come into the room. After that I had to sleep with my door ajar and Tigger disappeared. And by disappeared, I mean someone ran him over with a car and I was forced to look at the lifeless body in the street the next day and every day after that when leaving our house.

Once that came to light, it explained my night terrors of seeing a dark shadow in my doorway and the feeling of being paralyzed. The feelings of hating my body started to make sense. I felt ugly all over and like I had an invisible stain that wouldn't go away. It was a stain you can't scrub off no matter how hot the shower and no matter how hard you wash your body. Between that and the cigarette burns, it all started to click. The stain feeling was hard to shake but for the burns, one thing that made it easier for me was turning those scars into flowers with a gel pen. As it turns out those little marks are perfect for the inside details of a flower. When I did this, I saw beauty instead of a burn and since then it has helped me love my scars. I'd get told to stop drawing on myself all the time but never did and till this day I still do it. I wasn't hurting anyone by it and no one saw what I saw every time I looked at my knee or arm. Creating beauty out of something ugly made me feel better about showing my skin. Plus, a little flower above the knee is super cute if you ask me and honestly anyone who is upset over you drawing on yourself can hush. Here's why: firstly, it will wash off (just don't use sharpie), and secondly, every flower was a form of self-love, even if I didn't know it yet. The way I see it, the love that I give myself in those floral drawings and affirmations, when I look down and smile instead of frown, will help my love for myself grow and the scars and stain will continue to fade, and my body will be mine again. When that time comes, I will just be covered in flowers, and, to tell you the truth... I'm excited for that day.

Thoughts On The Drop Off

I started with this time of my life to force myself to be more open with y'all. The truth is, Robert and I faced a lot of other horrible things at the hands of Lynn and Junior, and I've never talked about it before this. Well, not in depth. What I've shared with y'all took a lot of confronting the evil head on and accepting it was part of my story. For the longest time I was ashamed of what we went through, and I avoided it like the plague. I avoided it so well that it started to feel like another person's story. I refused to accept it happened to me. It did though, and shame should have no part in accepting that, especially because I had no control over that whole situation: I was a kid. Robert and I were children that an older man took advantage of. We didn't put ourselves in that situation, we were born into it and thankfully saved from it by an act of courage from Lynn on a rainy night.

That type of decision couldn't have been easy for a mother to make. Or at least I'd hope not. I'm so thankful for that act of courage and insight from Lynn that night because it saved me from an angry man who hurt innocent children and who was my real boogeyman. If it weren't for her decision that night, I don't know where my life would have ended up, but I know it wouldn't be where I am now. Forgiveness didn't happen overnight; it took many years for me to get to that point, and for the longest time I told myself I hated Lynn and didn't want anything to do with her. Talk about mother issues, am I right. Therapy helped me realize that I don't want her to take my energy because I don't deserve that. Instead it was acceptance and indifference that set me free. The miracles of therapy are truly fantastic. It really is like a little light bulb goes off when you have a breakthrough. So instead, I thank her for having me and for dropping me off that night and I thank her for giving me a clear vision of what I never want in my life. And, I continue to dance.

Chapter 2

INTO THE FOSTER FUNNEL

2

FOSTER CARE

Before I dive into foster care, I need to state the obvious which is: all our stories are different. I don't mean to glam the system up because it is far from it, but I will say that foster care saved my life, and I will forever be thankful for the system and my foster parents, The Jacksons. There really should be more like them. I loved them like grandparents and my foster home was a loving environment. From the stories I've heard from other fosters this is not the case for a lot of kids. So, when I talk about foster care, please keep in mind that this is my experience. If someone comes to you and opens about theirs, let them talk, because trust me, it won't be the same.

Foster care is an interesting place. It's a melting pot of hurt children trying to overcome hardship in a place that isn't home. It's brave people wanting to make a better environment for children and opening up their homes. Both the kids and parents can learn from one another. It isn't your everyday All-American TV family household, or at least at the time. Instead, the halls are loud with children talking all at once. Kids are coming and going at any moment. It is chaos. You had to fight for food, fight for your chance to play a game, and then there were actual fights that erupted at any given moment. Have you seen the movie *Heavyweights* with Ben Stiller? Take that energy into my foster home but minus the starving-the-kids part. It was a summer camp that sometimes turned into *Lord of The Flies* amongst the children when the adults weren't looking. If you pushed the wrong person like I did over a well-earned bag of gummy bears you could end up with a vacuum being smashed against your head; while having a dent in my head makes for a good icebreaker now, I also learned a lot that day. Some kids like myself learned quickly to be quiet and not start anything because some children were extremely angry and a lot stronger. There where kids who started fights on purpose to test the boundaries and see what they could get away with in the home. When that happened, most of us would step to the side and observe the outcome. A lot of the time those kids were transferred out, never to be seen again.

The day Robert and I arrived at the Jacksons' house is still one of those memories that plays in my head in perfect full-color. They lived in a cul-de-sac that separated their neighbor's house with wooden fencing on the sides and a sun-faded black fence out front. Inside the yard were bikes and toys scattered everywhere. We arrived in the summer and as I grabbed my things from the car and walked towards the front door, I could hear kids screaming and laughing from the backyard. When Ms. June opened the door, she had the biggest smile on her face, and it just filled you like a hug. She invited us in and took us straight to the backyard. There were tons of people: kids playing in the pool, in the playhouse, and hanging out in the hot tub. Ms. June's husband, Pappers, was sitting under the porch cutting up watermelon and beckoned us over to have some. This moment is how I believe summers should be, just add a frozen Capri-Sun to the mix and you're set!

Shortly after arriving Ms. June asked a few kids to give us a tour and show us to our rooms. The girl's bedroom was the largest room in the house and could fit four bunk beds. This is where I would be staying. So, I put my trash bag on my bunk and the tour continued. On the other side of the house is where the boys stayed. Since there weren't that many of them, they had two separate rooms across the house which also consisted of bunkbeds. That is where Robert stayed. The Jacksons' son, TJ, had his own bedroom on the boy's side. The Jacksons adopted TJ when he was an infant even though they were an older couple and had grandchildren of their own – they couldn't say no to that cute little face. TJ pretty much ruled the house when the Jacksons weren't in sight – when it came to the kind of games we'd play, it was his way or the high way. Personally, I loved his games. They always involved army outfits and challenges that tested our skills and abilities. If you weren't playing to win were you even playing?

As the tour reached the backyard, Robert and I discovered that Pappers had built a huge playhouse there that included a tree swing that curved from the playhouse rooftop across a big magnolia tree. When we had the goat, this game turned into survival-mode when that jerk of a beast charged at you. As someone who loves all animals with the only exception of goats, I blame that dude for giving the others a bad rep. Pappers also had a woodshed where he taught the boys to work with their hands. Even though it was a boys-only place, he would let me in to play with the tools occasionally and I think that's the reason why I love being in Lowes so much. The smell of wood and saw dust transports me back to those days. Over the pool, Pappers hung two ropes above one another and kids would have contests to see who could hold on the longest. Not to brag or anything but I was pretty good and would wrap my whole body around the top rope as my final move. It was a kid's dream backyard that included a goat, dogs, and cats galore. I was thrilled to play but right when we were about to run into the new paradise, I felt my head forced downward and before I knew what was happening my face was slammed into a toy chess set by one of the boys as he welcomed us to Foster Care.

I laugh at this memory now because it really does sum up the rude awakening that foster care was for me. Plus, the kid who slammed my head into the toy chess later became one of my favorite people, who I still keep in contact with through social media. He is doing great if you were wondering and has shaken that particular habit of welcoming people.

It was a tough first year in the system. Having a home filled with five or more kids at any given time meant there were always games to be played, races to be had, and matches to be won. Most of the time we all loved playing together, but you learned quickly not to get too close to anyone because they could be gone the next day. Robert and I saw so many kids rotated out that we assumed it would happen to us soon. All of the emotions from the abuse and transitioning into a new life took a toll on us both, but I expressed it differently than Robert. I kept everything in and would explode in breakdowns that involved me throwing everything I had away and crying for hours. That was my way of disappearing. Robert, however, expressed his turbulent emotions through angry, often physically violent, outbursts. He would end up in fights with other kids in the home and at school. His episodes got worse after the state allowed us one-hour visits with our birth mom Lynn, and they eventually had to transfer him to a special facility that focused on children with behavioral issues. They put all his visits with Lynn on hold.

The day he left felt like a dream. It was the first time in my seven years of life that I didn't have Robert by my side. He protected me the best he could during all those years of abuse and in the blink of an eye he was gone. I broke down and threw all my clothes and personal items over the neighbor's fence. Only after crying and hiding under the bed for an hour did I have to go pick it all up. A social worker came to the house a few days later to help me talk about how I felt.

After that day I had scheduled visits with Robert and Lynn at different times every few months. They would bring us into a monitored room, and we could play or talk. Robert and I mostly colored or drew pictures. He showed me the correct way to use a crayon and how to get the perfect shading, which I still think about when using color pencils. The visits with Lynn were cancelled most of the time, or she'd sit and smoke and make promises of returning home. One visit she even brought Junior, thinking I had missed him. That was shut down real fast when Junior gave me a forever ring and my Supervisor asked if I wanted to leave. The visits with Lynn and Robert went on for about a year but that came to a stop when Robert's emotional state continued to worsen after visits. He would relapse into an angry stage and hurt others after the visit was over. In order to keep him from having episodes, they put our visitations on hold too.

As for Lynn, our visits stopped the day I wore my best dress. It was a summer day and for some reason just Ms. June and I were at the house. As I got ready, I put on my favorite dress. It was black on the bottom and white on top with a daisy flower pattern design that went across the chest to break up the colors. Ms. June had just helped me put on my puffy dress socks when the phone rang, and she left to answer it. I could hear talking and something in me just knew Lynn was cancelling our visit but this time it was forever. I sat on a red chair listening from the other room as Ms. June begged her to not cancel.

After the phone call ended Ms. June entered the room and by that time I was already curled up in a ball and crying. I don't know how I knew but I did. Something inside me told me and that hurt more than any punch or cigarette burn ever did. So, for the first time, I let my guard down. That was when Ms. June picked me up, took me to the rocking chair and held me as I broke down.

My social worker came over a few weeks later and said she had a surprise for me. She came up the driveway with a giant smile and holding a teddy bear with a bow tie. She told me that Junior wasn't my dad, and I would not be seeing him ever again. After he found out I wasn't his, Lynn gave up parental rights and that teddy bear was like a new beginning. I named him Beary because I was a child and thought it was so clever. When he's feeling fancy, it's Mr. Beary. I still have him to this day and every time I look at him, I smile. That day was a blessing.

When they separated Robert and I, our lives went in two different directions. Robert was living a childhood of pills that numbed him and he survived by holding on to the idea that Lynn was coming back. Lynn made a lot of promises to us about returning home and Robert didn't get to see all the canceled visits like I did which is why, I believe, he held on to that hope. I was living in a good home and learning that there was a better life out there than the one we lived before. I survived on knowing that I never wanted to be like Lynn or to feel that pain again.

The longer I stayed at the Jacksons' the easier it was – easier than I had thought it would be – to forget Lynn. Although things were chaotic in the home, it was also filled with laughter and family activities. Most of all, it was filled with love. I became close with the kids who were there, and our days involved being outside making pirate ships with Randy or recreating Spice Girls dances with Rosalynn and Sheena until we heard the dinner bell. The Jacksons were an older couple who had kids of their own and grandkids who would come over and hang out. I became super close with their granddaughter, who was a year older than me. We were two peas in a pod! Two amigos causing a ruckus in the kitchen and going on backyard adventures. During the summers I would stay the night at her house where we'd play barbies and watch the movies I wasn't allowed to watch at the Jacksons. She was my best friend and her brother treated me like a little sister, which meant telling me dragonflies ate people and that elevators with a hole in the door were haunted by the person who was shot. He also taught us that playing pool is all about geometry and if you knew math then you had it in the bag. As someone who is no math champion, I can concur that I suck at pool as well, so maybe he was right.

The one thing that the Jacksons did that changed everything though, was buying us kids our own personal trunks to keep our belongings in instead of trash bags. I still have mine till this day and I don't think I will ever get rid of it. It reminds me of where I am from and how much has changed. The Jacksons invested in the foster kids they could take into their home. We were taught manners and that you said yes ma'am and no sir and that there better not be elbows on the dinner table. We went to church twice a week, our family outings were going on camping trips and exploring the local springs and, as for summers, that meant learning to ride horses, dancing, or having war head contests at the local summer camp. We'd fill our mouths with four or five of the sourest black candy at a time and see who could last the longest before spitting them out from our cheeks. The summer that will forever be my favorite is the beach trip where I discovered my love for seagulls. I somehow got my hands on a disposable camera and went straight to work with documenting every seagull I could. They are so majestic! When Ms. June picked up the film her immediate reaction was to say, "Who let Patricia have the camera." I like to think I could have been a bird photographer if they had invested in my great eye, but sometimes unanswered prayers are best in the end.

It wasn't just summers that the Jacksons invested in us either: they created a daily routine out of chaos that involved shower routines and homework hours. We were expected to help around the house because when everyone did their part it made things easier in the home.

Ms. June loved crafts and would always have us creating something, whether it was tomb stones for the front yard on Halloween or making homemade birthday cakes as a group. When we weren't in school Ms. June and Pappers would make French toast on Saturdays and us kids were allowed to roam the neighborhoods. When it was time to come home, she would ring this huge dinner bell that hung on the front porch. I am totally having one of these for my kids, I don't care if it looks crazy! Until then, going inside the house was almost like a sin. If we could be outside, then we were expected to be outside, and I was okay with that. As a child I was a mix between a tomboy and a girlie girl. I felt most myself playing in the yard with dirt on my hands dressed in a swimsuit and princess jewelry. The outside world had adventure written all over it and I wanted to be a part of it all, as long as I looked my best.

Our dinners were almost always home cooked because it was easier to feed an army on a homecooked meal than with take-out. Everyone would get a plate and it was first come first serve. Which meant if you wanted seconds, you better eat fast. We all sat at a large wooden farmhouse table that could seat at least ten of us and between everyone reaching and grabbing and talking, it was a wild mess of awesomeness. We all sat on a wooden bench which resulted in a lot of sliding back and forth as people reached over you. After we thanked the Lord for our daily bread we would feast! Luckily the Jacksons didn't have a strict rule when it came to meals, like you had to finish what was on your plate. Their one food rule was you at least had to take a bite of your dinner. I hated tuna so much that I once fell asleep at the table because I refused to eat it. My first hunger strike and of course I fell asleep! I can't even remember what happened next, but

I'd like to think that I was carried to my bed while the other kids applauded me for sticking it to the man.

The longer I stayed there the more they lightened up on me and bent the rules a bit. On French Toast Saturdays Pappers would save me a plate in the fridge if I slept past breakfast and there weren't many kids in the home. Sometimes there would only be four or five of us max and when everyone was playing or doing something else, I would ask Ms. June to go swimming. It took a lot of convincing her I was okay to swim by myself and that she could watch me from the kitchen window. Of course, the day I finally got her to say yes, TJ wanted me to play WWE-takes-over-Jurassic-Park with him. By the time I had put on my suit and started talking to TJ the pool broke. There was a slit somewhere and the whole pool crashed open. If I had been swimming Ms. June said I would have been pressed up against the fence under the deck and could have drowned. I was never allowed to swim by myself again after that and the Jacksons made sure to buy a sturdier pool.

One of my favorite experiences in foster care was getting picked to participate in a Toys"R"Us shopping spree. I imagine they picked it out of a hat but to make it more interesting let's say they saw my awesome race skills and knew I was the girl for the job, or so they thought. I had to wake up early that day. My social worker and I were there before the sun rose and they had all of us kids line up with a shopping cart and then hit a timer which meant to run throughout the whole store as fast as you could and just grab as many things as you can. Well, my little self-wanted to make sure I picked out toys I knew other kids would like in the home and went around slowly talking items out with my social worker. At one point I think she realized I'd do it for every item and told me we were in a race and that I could just grab and go. I understood what she was saying but I wanted to make it personal, so we faced some challenges. I was able to get every kid in the home something and snagged myself a CD player that said "good morning" when you opened it. I listened to 98 Degrees on repeat for a whole month after that.

 If I could go back and relive this as an adult, I'd still agree with little me about getting gifts that are meaningful, however I'd approach it differently. If I did this as an adult, I'd research the store isles and memorize where everything was and then make a map in my head on the quickest way around the store to accomplish such task in a certain time frame. It's called improving your method!

In fourth grade I discovered my worth and that being a foster kid was, apparently, a bad thing. At the Jacksons everything was great, and I was happy. I loved being a part of their home, but they were just my foster parents and the kids on the school bus made sure to remind us. The Jacksons sent us to a public school that required uniforms unless you were a fifth grader. I had to pick between either a red, white or blue shirt to go with a pair of navy blue or khaki shorts, pants, or skort. The one time it was acceptable to wear regular clothes was on your birthday. I made sure to rock my bell bottoms when given the chance. I even hid my Tamagotchi in one of the pant pockets. I felt so cool! My point is, we all wore uniforms, so it wasn't like we were going to school in rags like in the movie *Annie*. Instead, it was like we had a stamp on our head that said Foster Kid. The kids on the bus would play jokes on us like telling us our foster parents were waiting in the front office to pick us up and then laugh at us as we ran after the bus when we realized they had lied. The day I ran after the bus with a younger kid on my hip was the first time in my life that I realized were I stood in the world and the crappy part about it was I had no control over it. Surprisingly though, the bullying was only on the bus or at least it was for me. None of my classmates cared or maybe they didn't know but either way they were nice. Other than the bus ride I loved being at school and learning. My favorite teacher was Mrs. Weaver, who was beautiful; she was tall with curly brown hair that went to past her shoulders. She was younger than our other teachers and a lot kinder. She liked me too and would always ask if she could use my items to demonstrate the assignment. Until one day, she asked to use my purple ruler to go over the rules on how to properly use one. As she went to bend it a bit to prove it was not something you bent... SNAP! She broke my favorite purple ruler, and I was forced to use a wooden one. I'm not trying to say I'm still bitter about it, but I will say she never replaced it.

One day during P.E. I met a boy named Chad. He had dark hair, freckles, and a broken leg in a cast. He was forced to stay under the pavilion because of his injury. Luckily that was one of my favorite spots other than the tetherball area. The pavilion had a lot of games, like hula hoop, but my favorite thing to do during P.E. was destroy my knuckles and play on the Connect-A-Scooter. That day I asked Chad if he'd like to join, and he said yes! We pretty much fell in love racing to see who was the fastest. He was my first real crush. Then one day Chad decided he had a crush on a fifth grader and would have his friend Tommy tell me through a note at lunch. When I saw him holding hands with the blonde girl who rode my bus I was crushed. His new girlfriend was the girl who made every bus ride miserable. She was a cool girl who wore Hanson shirts and rode in the back of the bus. Her and Chad ended up going to the fifth-grade dance together and she continued to pick on me until the end of year. I think what really broke my heart about the situation was the dance. It was a 1950s themed dance and the girls got to wear poodle skirts. I wanted to wear one so bad.

The dramatic heartbreak from Chad was easy to get over but what she did wasn't. The words she said and the way she made me feel were drilled into me five days a week and that isn't easy to brush off. It's weird the things we remember about people, especially the ones who hurt us. One thing that has helped me move forward over the years was writing her letters and this one, my friends, is the last.

TO THE I LOVE YOU BULLY

Every morning the bus picked you up and you waved goodbye to your mom saying "I love you" in sign language only to turn around and tell me, "You'll never have a mom to say I love you to." You were wrong, I found the best mom in the world, and she loved me more than anything I could have ever imagined. She also taught me to put my trust in God when dealing with mean girls. The bible tells us that we are blessed if we don't walk along with people who are wicked and I am so proud of myself for learning early on the type of person I wanted to surround myself with. I thank you for that. Over the years I discovered how important it is to love myself and not let someone else tell me my worth. I know I am strong, resilient, and that when I start my family to make sure my children know kindness wins; that you lend a hand to help those who have less than you rather than kick them when they are down. I am sorry that you didn't learn that from your family, and I hope you never have to wipe the tears from your kids face when someone makes fun of them for something you couldn't provide. What you had with your mom was beautiful and I did want it. Thankfully I received it, but a lot of kids in the system don't, and if you somehow find this letter all I ask is that you give back to them. Their names are on the Christmas trees you see in the store during the holidays, and the system is always looking for donations to help those kids have somewhat of a normal childhood. Give to them. Open your heart and get to know those kids' stories because they're not all the same. But no matter their history, they all deserve love. The last thing I have to say to you is that I hope you are happy and loved and I mean that with all my heart. I don't wish anything bad on you anymore and I'm sorry I did because I realize that was wrong. Getting revenge on you wouldn't fix anything and in fact probably would make me feel worse. If anything, I don't want that for myself, so instead I forgive you and hope you can open your heart to people who are different to you, and maybe even to the foster world.

> Warmly,
> Patricia

Thoughts on Foster Care

Again, it is not a place that should be glammed up and I was truly fortunate to be placed at the Jacksons'. They created a special place in my heart that I will be forever grateful for. I can't express how thankful I am for their love, the caring environment, and safety they provided me at a time I didn't think existed.

With that said, it was foster care, and the experience leading up to their house was terrifying. We were being moved from one place to another and had no stability. For a child to be thrown into that type of system is traumatizing. Although I was no longer being abused, I was still learning and seeing how the system packs kids up and moves them without preparing them and without talking to the other children or providing some sort of support or understanding. That is scary for a child not to know what's going on and it created feelings that built up inside that I had no idea how to talk about because I didn't know the words to describe them. The one emotion that I did understand was joy. I wrapped myself around that feeling so hard because it was the only thing I understood and felt comfortable around. But, the truth is I hid under the bed that day and cried from fear of being taken away, and up until this day I'm still working on helping that little girl feel safe enough to make herself heard.

At the time, I had no idea that the scared feeling of being tossed out at any moment was an actual thing people felt because no one talked to me about it. For me, it added on to the trauma from Junior and Lynn. While I was living in a better place, I was still very much afraid of being sent away at any moment and a child shouldn't have to face the battle of being accepted for just existing the best they can.

The Jacksons did their best and thankfully their best helped guide me in my later years but again, it's not like that for everyone and for the children who have gone through more abuse and hurt while in the system I am truly sorry. You didn't deserve that and still don't. You are not to blame for anything. Just like myself you were a child that was thrown into a world of chaos and for some that chaos came with more violence, uncertainty, and anger like Robert. Just like that wasn't Robert's fault, it wasn't yours either and I hope you know that.

Chapter 3
THE JOYS OF A NAME

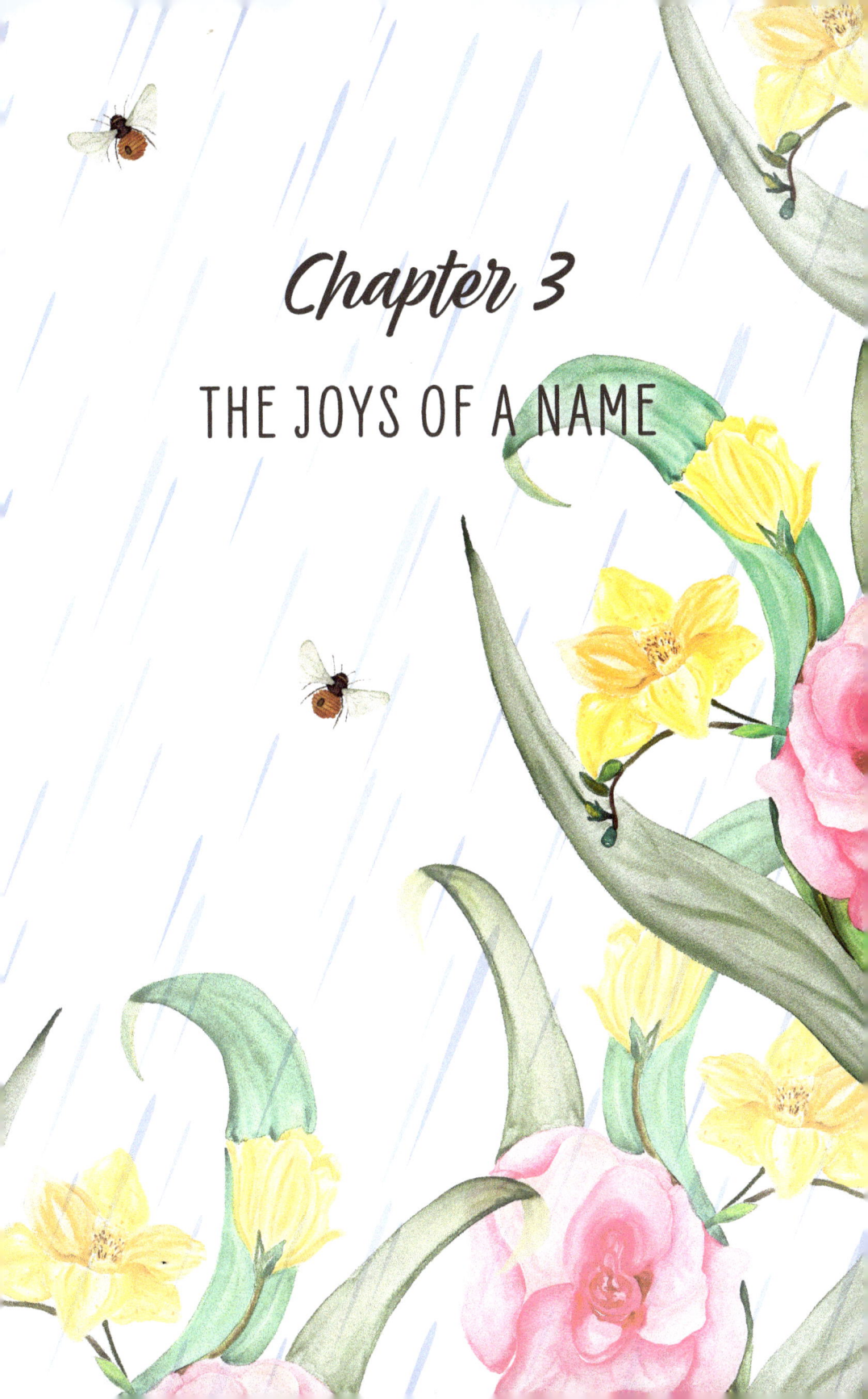

3

ADOPTION

Everything changed after fourth grade: that summer the Jacksons rented a lake house on Bear Lake. It was there that I learned to fish and that worms have more than one heart. That day the weather was overcast, and the water was flat. There was another kid on the dock, and we were hanging out when Pappers walked up behind us with fishing poles and a tackle box. He had us look inside this little plastic container the held live worms and encouraged us to pick them up with our hands. He then helped us hook the worms up to the hook. A good tip he taught us was when you go to place them on the hook you must make sure not to puncture their hearts. I didn't catch a darn thing but the experience itself lives with me and, while I haven't fished with a worm in forever, it's still a fun tip for the kids.

By mid-summer, my tetherball skills were becoming incredible, Chad was long gone, and Ms. June let me paint the inside of the shed. I fell in love with painting after receiving a paint set at a holiday foster gathering. Santa walked around and gave every kid one present and mine, mine was the best. It was a watercolor set that came with a brush! Did I know that? Nope. I had no idea what I was looking at but after learning what I could create from those colors, I never wanted to stop. I painted everything Ms. June would let me, so when she asked me to help paint the shed, I felt honored. We had to clean it first, which involved lots of bleach and stripping the old wallpaper. It was a tiny room that had so much potential. That shed ended up being our refuge, where we would have snacks and juice packs while playing outside. Ms. June and I painted it bright yellow with white counters – it was so cute! The finishing touch included two gigantic pots we found while driving around. We placed them under the window that opened towards the lake.

Like every summer before that the Jacksons had friends and family over frequently. The summer day I met with Ann and Courtney by myself was one for the books. I had woken up earlier than the other kids that day, tiptoeing over the sleeping bodies on the living room floor towards the Poptarts in the kitchen. You can't have a day of adventure on an empty stomach! The table still had dominos scattered everywhere from the game the night before, and looking beyond the morning dew on the windows, I could see a few adults sitting outside by the lake. The benefits of waking up with the adults is coffee; by the time I was nine I was drinking a cup of milk and a splash of joe whenever I got the chance. The downfall of waking up with adults is they kindly ask you to help pick up the place and demand that you shower before exploring. By the time I had taken out the trash and showered, a few of the other kids were up and already outside in the water. I threw on my swimsuit and began another day of cannon balls off the dock and taking turns on the tube. By lunch time I had just finished destroying one of the boys at tetherball when Ann and Courtney called me over. With all the fun going around I didn't see them arrive or I was just used to their presence so I didn't notice. Ann and Courtney were always around since Ann worked for The Department of Children and Families. They called me over to one of the yard chairs and asked if I'd like to stay with them for a while. By this point I didn't think I was ever leaving the Jacksons' and figured I'd stay with them for a few weeks, so I said yeah. I didn't think anything of it. Ann said they'd be back in a few days to pick me up. Before I left to stay with them, Pappers took me to see my first movie in theaters. It was *Star Wars Episode I*: I was blown away that something like a movie theater even existed! Never in my life had I seen a movie on a screen that big and even though *Star Wars Episode I* is considered the worst in the franchise, I still love it. At the time I didn't know it but that was Pappers' way of saying goodbye to me. I will forever be thankful for him because he was the closest thing I had to a father figure in my early life. I like to think my love for sawdust, adventure, and nerdy things like bugs and insects, space, and *Star Wars* came from him. I don't know if that's weird, but I lived with the Jacksons' for four years and picked up a lot of their behaviors, and after leaving their place some of them were hard to shake. Poor Ann was in for a treat.

The day Ann and Courtney picked me up they took my trunk that had all my belongings and placed it in their car, and I said goodbye to Ms. June and Pappers not realizing it was the last time I'd live with them. You would think it would've clicked when they were helping me pack my trunk and giving me photos of my time there, but what can I say, sometimes things fall into place a bit slower for me. Looking back at this time, I wish I would have taken one more look at my room and the foster home. You know, have a proper goodbye.

The car ride to Ann's place involved a lot of conversation but the feeling of motion sickness makes up most of that memory. I had a horrible history of throwing up in cars that resulted in punishment before foster care and later on, annoying everyone in foster care.

My main goal was to not throw up – thankfully the car ride wasn't too long. They lived in a townhouse in a partially gated community. When you entered their home, it opened to a hallway with an atrium to the left. I tried to get Ann to make this a shark tank for years, but she never budged. The front of the home had two bedrooms and a bathroom. That would be the youth territory. It would be the first time in years that I had my own room. Ann told me everything in that room was mine and that if I wanted to redo it I could. The room was pretty and had a lot of natural light. Best of all, it belonged to me. It was an odd feeling, but at the same time exciting. To be taken away from a home of chaos and invited into a home that felt eerily quiet when walking into for the first time was overwhelming. Then, the first night there, Ann played Barbies with me. She put Ken in the best ball gown I had and made him dance. It was so goofy, and I liked it, so we put all the boys in dresses. That night, with the half-unpacked trunk and my new, unfamiliar surroundings as their backdrop, our barbies had a drag prom.

Ann's house was quiet compared to the Jacksons' and as the days went by, I felt alone and missed foster care. I missed climbing the magnolia tree in the backyard and watching the cars in traffic; playing with the white flowers around the pool that leaked sticky white liquid and the bees with the big booty and small wings. I missed the loud noise of kids throughout the house, and my friends. It was the first time I truly felt alone. Ann was amazing though and let me call Ms. June every night to share how my day went; that continued for a few weeks. Bless Ms. June for answering and for Ann for understanding, even though some nights they stayed on the phone talking. Ann was probably questioning why Ms. June didn't tell her I was loco. Adjusting to a new home brought a lot of challenges for us all. Both Courtney and

Ann were on completely different schedules and slept in super late. Whereas I was up, hungry, and ready for the day with the sun. Ann started to joke that she could tell when I was awake because she'd hear the toilet flush and fridge open. I didn't mind, she was right. I wake up to whale songs happening in my stomach and if they aren't fed, things will get ugly. That part was weird to me, though: breakfast was always ready for us at the Jacksons' and if we slept past it we knew there was cereal. My new home didn't have that system in place, and I soon realized that if I wanted food other than cereal I would have to try and make it or figure it out myself.

One of the biggest challenges we faced was communication. After telling Ann we didn't do chores at the Jacksons' she made a phone call which resulted in her explaining to me that when we were asked to help around the house, we were doing chores.

I felted tricked.

Between adapting to a new routine and feeling a bit of culture shock, learning to separate the white from reds was at the bottom of my to do list.

Ann did keep Ms. June's dinner rule which was nice since going from a loud dinner table environment into a quiet three-person conversation sitting at a round table was awkward in the beginning. I was used to elbowing the kid next to me, fighting for space and food, not politely asking for more water. Ann learned that I ate only one thing at a time, in a circular motion. If my food touched, I didn't want it. She handled my approach to food very well and defended me when her dad came down for a visit and yelled at me for eating too slow. He was a military man who would yell at us kids to stop slamming doors while he watched baseball on the TV on mute and listened to it on the radio. He was scary at first, but once I got to know him I couldn't wait to sit next to him and act like I knew what was going on in the baseball world. I thought he was awesome.

While it was quiet in the home, I did love having a new sister. Courtney was almost five years older than me which made her instantly cool in my book. When she and Ann would visit the foster home, every kid wanted Courtney's attention. She was the badass older sister to everyone. Rumor has it that another girl at the home was supposed to be adopted, but her dad came into the picture, and she went off the market, so they came back looking and found me. Talk about luck! Courtney was pretty, with shoulder length dirty blonde hair. She was a mixture of a young Reese Witherspoon and Julia Roberts in looks. She would take a bullet for me and the people she loved; she was protective and strong, and not to mention a bit disturbed, but aren't we all. I don't know her full story but from what I heard her birth mother had five other children and just dropped Courtney off because she was troubled. She was also adopted by Ann when she was ten. I'm not sure of when she entered the system, but Ann found her and they connected. Her adoption story is so cute. She apparently was always at the Department of Children and Families and would stand in Ann's office doorway and ask her every time if she could adopt her until one day Ann said yes. That's what I call tenacity! By the time I came around, she'd had Ann to herself for five years and you could tell what a great bond they had created. Ann would tell a story about a boy walking down the beach after a hurricane and throwing all the washed-ashore starfish back into the ocean, when a man approached him and said, "You know you can't save them all, right?" To which the little boy responded, "Yeah but I can at least save one." That was their bond in a nutshell; Courtney wore a starfish necklace around her neck every day.

By the time I came into the family, she was almost in high school and wore punk rock shirts, played soccer and was a part of Junior

Reserve Official Training Camp. In the late morning she would wake up and do 100 push-ups and sit ups before starting her day, which, most of the time, was more climbing trees and going mudding with her friends. She didn't eat breakfast – which I consider a sin – and she survived off Mountain Dew and Doritos. I don't think I ever saw her eat breakfast or lunch now that I'm thinking about it. She mostly snacked and ate a dinner for five in one sitting, only to then have seconds a few hours later. It was impressive.

We lived in a neighborhood that had a community pool, and that is where Courtney and I bonded. We loved pool games and she was always down to play, often inviting her friends to join us. A few things Courtney and I had in common were: we loved being outside, WWE, and the water. At the Jacksons' we were banned from watching WWE after a few of us turned TJ's room into a wrestling ring. Now I had the freedom to be body slammed by Courtney all day, and she took pleasure in doing it, but would yell at me for laughing as I went under the water. We'd play shark and Minos, categories, and had jumping contests. You know, the classic pool games. She showed me how to do a back dive but couldn't teach me a backflip – my legs just don't tuck. It was the perfect way to end the summer.

As the summer was coming to an end, Ann started to dive further into details on the adoption process. She said that she wanted to be my new mom and that if I liked it here after 90 days, it would be my permanent home. By then, I had an idea this was going to be my permanent home because we were going to weekly classes with other new parents and foster kids. The counselors talked about our feelings and opening up emotionally to our new family. Those weekly classes were fun and helped with the transition a bit. I came away from them with the movie *Stuart Little* burned into my retinas. It's adorable, and loved by the adoption community because it teaches children that it's okay to not look like the rest of your family and be different.

Another take away from those classes was the box metaphor. The counselors had us all get inside a box; we had to close the top, open it back up and then look around. The box represented the emotional walls we created for ourselves and that in order to genuinely connect with those around us, parts of the walls were going to have to start coming down. A great message if you ask me, but busting through the cardboard box was a lot easier than the invisible force field made of suffering and fear that surrounded me. But, I liked the message! I also liked the idea of having a permanent home, but not the idea of calling Ann "mom." That word didn't make sense to me. So, Ann let me call her Ann until I felt comfortable and said I never had to call her mom if I didn't want to.

Once summer had finally said goodbye and August graced us with tax-free weekends and school shopping, I started at a new school closer to Ann's place. It was walking distance so there wasn't a bus stop, but instead of walking there myself Ann drove me. After school I'd stay with her friends who were another foster family that lived down the road. They were the Mixers, a family made up of ten adopted kids. The night I met them I felt at home; it reminded me of the Jacksons' place. There were kids in the pool and running around the yard and the best thing was there wasn't a quiet spot in the house. I threw on my swimsuit and joined the fun. As I was swimming in the pool a young girl swam up to me and said, "Your mother loves me more than you." Before I realized what I was saying, the words, "That's funny because she's adopting me," came out of my mouth and I swam away. At the Jacksons' that type of remark would have ended in my head underwater fighting for my life. Things really were changing and I was looking forward to going over to the Mixers' place after school.

The thing I didn't look forward to was school itself. The anxiety of starting a new school took over my thoughts. In the days leading up to the first day we went shopping and I had laid out an outfit for every day of the week. This was my way of controlling the situation and it would be my first time without a uniform, so I wanted to look good. The first day I wore my new blue jumpsuit and black choker, trying to unlock my inner Sporty Spice. After being dropped off I walked to the pavilion and located my teachers X on the floor to line up. I was the first person there and felt so relieved! Other classes had kids sitting in line who were talking and laughing. As I was looking around a girl named Shannon was the first to introduce herself to me. If sunshine was a person, it would be her. She had blonde hair and was bright red from being sunburned on a family cruise over the summer. She took me under her wing and invited me into her group. I loved it. Her friends were cool and completely different from my previous school. I didn't want them to not like me and became so afraid of being found out that I kept my mouth shut about being a foster kid and started calling Ann "mom" only at school. Shannon and her friends liked swinging on the swings as high as they could while screaming "Papa Roach" on the top of their lungs. They did fun things like have murder mystery sleep overs and watch horror movies. They were smart and knew things I had no idea about, like who the heck was Harry Potter and some dude named Indiana Jones. Discovering the *Harry Potter* movies was one of the best things. I had just started reading the books but being able to see that a kid who was a misfit could have a chance of a great life gave me hope. Secretly I wished I was a wizard. To be a wizard would give me some explanation of why I went through all of those traumatizing experiences. Maybe that was my chance of getting powers. A silly thought but one that I still secretly wished happened.

Shannon and her friends liked to cause a ruckus and would stand up for what they believed in, which led to Shannon and I marching up to the front office and presenting a well thought out plan to give kids with summer birthdays pencils since their names were never on the morning announcements. This was a topic that had been ignored at my previous school and was now the same was happening here; I felt very strongly about it. Luckily Shannon understood my point of view. Maybe it was because she had an August birthday too, but anyway, despite the front desk lady seeming unimpressed with our well thought out plan, she said she would pass it on the principle. I should probably take that up with her and make sure she followed through. I mean, she's had plenty of time if you ask me.

My new school was awesome, and the kids were even cooler. The change to a new school had been better than I expected, and the months were flying by. I had stopped calling Ms. June and made friends with the neighborhood boys. Before I knew it, November had graced us with cooler weather. A few weeks leading up to the adoption court date Ann asked me if I wanted to keep my name or change it since I would be getting a new last name. At this time, I was obsessed with the names Gabriella and Isabella and wanted to go by Gabby or Izzy, so I pushed to have those as my first name. Ann said I should consider keeping my first name and focus on changing my middle name. That way I had something to remember my past. At the time I hated the idea and wanted to forget everything about my past but didn't want to argue. We settled on Elizabeth which was perfect because it was Ann's mother's name. Then on November 17, 2000, I became Patricia Elizabeth Sheridan. I remember feeling so excited, and the process went by in a blur.

The next day at school our teacher introduced a new student. As she said my name, my stomach dropped. How could she tell everyone without asking me first; I thought we liked each other and now she was announcing for all the fifth-grade class to hear that I was adopted! I did so well at keeping it quiet and within seconds all of that hard work was gone. I sat there in fear waiting for the other kids to turn and start making fun of me. Instead of an angry mob with pitch forks all the kids were curious, and thought being adopted was a cool thing because I was able to pick my parents. They acted completely differently to what I expected them to. When I went home and I told Ann what happened she said good, being adopted is a cool thing and I should be proud. I was proud and turned adoption into my fun fact. Of course, she took it further and reminded me why it was important to stay humble and kind. She talked about how beautiful of a thing adoption was and while I should be proud, I should never stop helping those less fortune now that I had the chance. She talked about how many older kids don't get adopted and, once they grow out of the system they are forgotten about; that I was very fortunate to be adopted at ten. She told me that my name would no longer be on the white rolled up paper with a red bow people see on Christmas trees in grocery stores – something about that hit hard. I had a family and a new name to go with it; we were the ones taking those papers home and playing Santa. That was weird.

By Christmas time I was calling Ann "mom" even after school.

After my adoption date my teacher had us do a class assignment about our family tree and heritage. This was an interesting subject to approach. As it turned out we had no idea what my heritage was. Ann and her family were the blondest, bluest-eyed Irish folks you could find. The idea of me being Mexican was thrown out along with Italian and Portuguese. When I wasn't in the sun, I could pass for Italian but the moment this body got vitamin D there was no hiding I was something else. My tan wasn't the beautiful olive glow that most Italians get; it was a dark red sun-kissed glow.

We decided to say I was Portuguese but would show my new family's background and explain how adoption works. The day that I presented my assignment in class I was tanner than any Irish person could ever get I'm sure, but I stood up and proudly talked about my family tree. As I was walking back to sit down a girl leaned over and whispered, "no one was paying attention to your speech, they were all distracted by your hairy legs."

I went to the Mixers' after school and cried about my legs. When my mom came to pick me up, she said I wasn't shaving my legs in fifth grade and could do it in middle school. Mrs. Mixer stood up for me and said if I was being made fun of, I should be allowed to shave. That night we went home, and Courtney introduced me to razors and shaving cream and taught me to beware of Nair. What lived under those hairy little legs were the cutest little calf muscles ever according to my mom. As she said, they were perfectly proportioned.

This experience was more than just shaving and discovering my perfectly proportioned calves though. It set a question in motion that I would ask myself for many years and that question was, "What am I?" I never questioned if I looked like anyone in my foster family because I thought that's how families work. For example, think of the 1997 film *Cinderella*, with Brandy in the lead role. You have a family and characters from different backgrounds and race and no one is questioning how Whoopi Goldberg and Victor Garber had a Filipino prince child. It just works. That's how foster care was. You were surrounded by so many different individuals, and you were family. Our backgrounds weren't a topic someone brought up and asked to put on a tree.

After the family tree assignment, I started to realize that not all families are like that and that was probably the message behind the ridiculous amount of *Stuart Little* comparisons. Dang it, why did I have to get distracted?! Darn you undiagnosed ADHD. Seriously though, I wasn't concerned if my new family looked like me or I them. I had new cousins who were dark haired and loved it and my mom and I would always laugh when someone said we looked alike and reply with, "It must be the eyes." My question was simply, "What am I?" and of course that caused me to think "Was there a country that everyone looked like me out there?"

As that question slowly started to eat at my thoughts, life sped up and before I knew it fifth grade was over, and we were celebrating my adoption with a Disney Cruise, along with my mom's friend Jane and her granddaughter Tess. Tess was an interesting child who loved all things oceanic and loved to explore rocks on the seawall. While my mom and Jane hung out, and Courtney explored the teen clubs, Tess and I snorkeled. We were out there for hours, and no one had to worry about us running off because we both couldn't get enough of the water and unlimited virgin piña coladas. Life was great. It was a new type of freedom, and I was enjoying every moment of it.

New Name Thoughts

So, fun fact about my adoption: I don't have a picture of the adoption court date because we never printed it out. My face looked like someone used the stupefy spell on me. My mom discovered many years later that the reason for that was because Courtney had told me that the judge would smack me the moment I was 'reborn'. Good times. Anyway, looking back at this time makes me think: holy cow little lady, what an emotional rollercoaster of fun and fear. A rollercoaster that blasted Vitamin C, 'Friends Forever' on the way down and Destiny's Child, 'Say My Name' on the way up. Once I knew what adoption was, I was loving it. The idea of getting a new family, new name, and a new place to live was a dream to me. It meant no one had to know I was a foster kid and, in a way, I felt like a spy. Who was I spying on? A little girl who felt like she didn't fit in even though she had a new home. My new life filled with happiness, a love that was still trying to be understood, and adventure that was unimaginable. It was like at any moment I would wake up and it would be over, but when that didn't happen, I felt like my past haunted me and would expose me for what was I was: a foster kid that didn't deserve a family or a mom to say I love you to. I wished I was like everyone else around me. To me, they never knew what it felt like to be exposed to horrible things at such a young age and I envied them for that. I wanted so badly to be like them. To be a normal kid. So, I became a spy and would make sure that little girl stayed hidden, masking myself for most of my childhood. I was happy but because of the new life that I wasn't waking up from I hid my feelings and pushed down my fears, so I felt isolated and lonely. My shadow man was still at my door and continued to be there the more I pushed my feelings down and tried to act like I was okay. He mocked my new life every time I looked at my door and I felt crazy for seeing him.

Earlier I mentioned learning to not get close to anyone in foster care because they could be gone the next day. While that is true, it is also a lie. You build relationships with familiar faces and kids who last as long as you. There's a bond there that never really breaks and when I couldn't turn to someone familiar, I had to rely on my thoughts to guide me instead. That transition led to me discovering a new type of loneliness.

So, to sum it all up, the whole experience was a hot mess of amazingness, sorrows, and growth for sure. There was an innocence that came along with my cluelessness in thinking adoption meant I no longer had to deal with my past and once I had a new family everything was good. I'm not sure if I'm the only one who felt that after adoption but for those of you who did, I want you to know the feeling of being afraid and like an imposter is normal and you don't have to face it by yourself. Trust me when I say talk to someone because the longer you push down the hurt child inside you, the more that child will scream until one day you can't push down their voice anymore. I hope you know to give your inner child their voice because they deserve to be heard too.

Chapter 4

THE HONEYMOON STAGE

4

The best word to describe my mom would be wonderful. She was a Miami-raised, green Camaro-driving badass. She pulled your focus without trying to whenever she entered a room. She had a great energy that could be described as something like Lucy from the sitcom *I Love Lucy* mixed with Michelle Obama. She was hilarious, with a quick wit, and had the biggest heart you could ever imagine. She truly loved children and felt her calling was helping keep them safe.

The way she poured her love into me will be one thing I am forever grateful for. From the moment I entered her home she invested fully into who I was to become. My reading level was below average and while Ms. June tried her best to help me, she also had seven or eight other kids at the same time that needed assistance with their homework; it was hard to focus on one child's needs when we all struggled. Every night of my fifth-grade year, my mom would have me sit on her lap and guide me through the *Chicken Soup* and *A Night Without Armor* books. I started with *Chicken Soup for the Kid's Soul* and slowly moved to reading preteens and teens as I went from fifth grade to middle school. By the time I was in seventh grade I was in regular classes and a hopeless romantic for poetry. As I got older, she continued to support my education and in particular nurtured my love for art. One thing Ms. June told her before adopting me was to keep me creating and she did just that; growing up I had access to any medium or wall in our house. She created an environment that helped me trust my own creative process and push myself further.

My mother worked for The Department of Children and Families and had dedicated her life to saving children. She knew how trauma affected the development of a child and what behaviors to expect from them. When I first entered her home, I was quiet, I didn't touch much and tried to become the best child she had ever known. Need me to run the dishwasher? Don't mind if I do. Is Dawn okay?

Yup, I'm that child.

By the time our 90 days came to an end, my poor mom had to replace the dishwasher, a window, and microwave. As much as I tried to be perfect, it never worked. I dropped everything, fell over my own feet, and misunderstood directions a lot. Which explains why she had me tested for ADHD in seventh grade.

Ann called this stage the "honeymoon stage", a stage where a child will try to come off as the perfect child. A people pleaser to be exact because they are afraid if they act up, they will be sent away. That type of mindset is built into foster care and hard to get rid of and coming from someone who is in the beginning stages of breaking the people pleaser mindset... it sucks. What's interesting about this stage is it can last the full 90 days that a child is with their soon-to-be adoptive parents (the "trail stage"). Then, when the child knows they are not going to be sent away, they start to feel safe and open up. That means all of the trauma, and anger, and plain ugly are coming out of the woodwork.

For me the honeymoon stage lasted until the beginning of sixth grade. A solid year of testing the water and observation. As soon as I felt safe that little box of trauma that was stored in my brain opened up. The night I had my first flashback, we were sitting in the living room having a family game night. I was wearing Courtney's *Powerpuff Girls* watch without asking and we started arguing. It wasn't anything crazy, the squabble ended when I gave her the watch back. But then, as our mom was getting up to go into the kitchen my brain translated her movement as her leaping to attack me. Something triggered my brain and I felt fear coursing throughout my body. It was the first time I had felt that afraid in years and my body did what it had always wanted to do in those terrifying moments, and that was run. A few hours later, I found myself standing on a stranger's porch in the middle of the night, asking to call my mom. I had no idea how I had ended up there, and I didn't remember running or walking for that long. When my mom came to pick me up, along with a couple of cop cars, she thanked the man for keeping me safe.

The next day she signed me up for therapy.

After that incident, my mom started talking to me more about what type of things I could expect later in life if I didn't talk out my problems in therapy. It wasn't a lecture, though; she was a pro at teaching me in a way that was genuine and interesting to me. Of course, I listened but that didn't mean I could fully comprehend her wise words when she said things like "You're going to be in your 30's trying to build a family and if you don't take care of this now it will all come out then." She was right though; I was a textbook case to her. Which is why I think she taught me as much as she could. She knew what to expect from me while I had no idea what to expect from myself.

That was the only flashback I experienced, but other things started happening in place of it. It was like my brain was finally connecting the dots of the events that happened from foster care and pre-foster care and the emotions that came with it felt fresh. At this time, I was visiting Robert a few times a year as he continued to change medicines and homes. Our visits were always pleasant from what I remember, but for the first time my brain showed me the truth when I looked at our photos. Robert was so drugged he couldn't keep his eyes open and there I was with a gift he picked out for me even though I was the one with a family. He loved me and would be over the moon when we saw each other. Emotions of guilt and unworthiness creeped in. I felt Robert should have been adopted instead of me. He was smarter, an innovative thinker, and had so much potential. The thought of how it wasn't right to waste a family on me kept occurring. Turns out that was survivors' guilt, a feeling I wouldn't be able to push down easily. As our visits continued, I was the one who started having outbursts. Once the visit was over and I would go into emotional breakdowns that would last a few days. As my brain continued to connect events, I started realizing why foster care was a sad place. There was a reason my friend Randy came back one more time to build a pirate ship with me before moving into the Ronald McDonald House. That one hit me hard. I was reading a poem about a boy with cancer and right in front of me it spelled out exactly what happened to Randy. I felt so stupid for not understanding sooner, and the fact that I didn't know if he made it crushed me. We never talked about the reason he was in the system, but I remember being angry at that thought. Knowing that he was in the care system with cancer was bullshit to me. I didn't understand how someone could not love him and how they could let him go through that alone. He was so precious and the best pirate ship builder on the block. The last day we hung out at the Jacksons', we build a pirate ship out of Styrofoam and then went on to have a talking contest. It drove everyone around us crazy; I'm pretty sure he won. He was competitive. Not knowing what happened still hurts. I think of him often and it is because of Randy that I will always donate to cancer research; his name will always be written on those hot air balloon stickers.

During this time of realization, not only were my emotions everywhere but I started having night terrors. They got to the point where I couldn't sleep without the lights on and would force myself to draw or redesign my room until I couldn't stay awake any longer. The dreams were the same every night. The black figure stood at my door while I lay frozen in my bed, unable to move or make a noise. Never once did I mention those to mom. I felt crazy and weak for being afraid of shadows in my dreams and instead would draw them out before throwing them away. The one time I was able to write how I felt in a poem made my mom cry, and said she wished she could take those feelings away. The poem was about being at a place of brokenness and suffocation, so I get why she cried, but after that I stopped writing my feelings down. I hated that I made her upset and didn't want her to feel that way because of me. She was already walking on eggshells at home. Courtney's birth mom stood her up for her birthday and she cried a lot, closed away in her room. Then there I was, a preteen growing up in the millennia, adding more trauma to the mix. Our home felt sad, and I could tell our mom was hurting too. I didn't like being touched and was only just warming up to hugs, but during this time all I wanted was the comfort of her arms around me; it was the one thing I could understand. She noticed this too and praised me like she always did when I showed progress. When we hugged it was it was my way of understanding her love for me; I felt temporarily grounded in a world of uncertainty and it helped me come back from a sea of emotions that filled my head. I think it helped strengthen our bond during this period.

It took some time for me to bond with Ann and it didn't happen all at once. It was a variety of things that built over time like physical affection and sharing feelings that were hard to explain normally. But the day I started to trust her was in sixth grade. My best friend and I had a friendship notebook that we exchanged with one another. It was filled with middle school drama and how horrible our lives were because we couldn't wear skull earrings or paint our nails black. Okay, and maybe some other drama thrown in there, but those middle school secrets aren't to be shared here.

That beautiful notebook was picked up by one of my teachers and read. She demanded a teacher conference and explained to my mom that the conversations I was having with my friend were inappropriate, and how I needed help. My mom calmly told my teacher that it was not her business to read the journal and once she had found out who it belonged to and noticed it wasn't school related, she should have respected my privacy. She defended me, and always said if we ever had a diary or journal, it was not hers to read and she'd respect it; that day she stood by her words. I remember feeling proud and looking at her differently after that. The second time that really brought us close was when we were walking around the shopping plaza waiting for Courtney to get off work, and we stopped outside the fitness center. The window looked in on treadmills and Ann jokingly dared me to throw my smoothie against it. She was crazy, I couldn't believe she told me to do that and told her no, that we could get in trouble. She walked away, calling me a chicken over her shoulder. Well, this girl is anything but and as she was walking away I not only threw that smoothie, but I chucked it with full force at the gym window. It vibrated off the glass noisily. Ann turned around and screamed,

"I was kidding, oh my gosh, run!"

She learned that day that I don't like being told I can't do something and that this girl ain't no chicken. We got back in the car, and both burst out laughing. That moment right there, that was when I truly knew I was safe.

Maybe if that magical moment never happened, the trauma box would have stayed shut and I could have avoided this hot mess, but here we are!

Once seventh grade came around everyone agreed we weren't getting anywhere in therapy without me talking. One thing I'm good at, my friends, is keeping things to myself, no matter how safe I feel. Therapy annoyed me; I didn't want to talk about the dolls and how they made me feel. I didn't want to talk about the man who hurt me and where he hurt me. I hated the way it made me feel and I had no idea how to express it in words, let alone trying to talk about something I didn't understand. I wanted to talk about the art on the walls. My therapist had two beautiful paintings hanging in her office. Both were from another patient of hers who had multiple personalities. Our therapy sessions mainly consisted of talking about her. I wanted to know what else she was painting and which one of her personalities painted. Was it the child, the shopaholic, or someone else I hadn't heard about? For me therapy was a chance to learn about someone else. If I talked about that person long enough it took the focus off me, or so I thought. Obviously, my therapist saw right through my plan and after trying everything in the book our visits came to an end, but not before doing the greatest thing in the world.

Getting rid of Junior.

FOREVER

She asked me to send Junior away to a place where he could never hurt me again. So that night we put Junior in an itchy suit that was filled with cockroaches, on the sun. That's right, I sent that guy to the sun in the worse travel outfit ever.

Take that you child abusing a-hole.

Once the therapy sessions ended, my mom took a different approach. She signed me up for dance classes – I would have stayed if I didn't see my first boys' lacrosse game by chance in the hall across from the studio. After that weekend, instead of buying new dance shoes, I looked for a mouth guard and cleats. Thursday Therapy nights turned into Saturday games and Panera hangouts with the family and Courtney's friends. My problems were still very much there but when I was active, it made things easier. As it turns out, playing a physical sport was exactly what I needed. It released anger I didn't know I had and helped me dissipate a lot of built-up energy. It was a great substitute for therapy, but my mom continued to use her secret ninja knowledge in a different way to help me prepare for life. She would encourage me to read the books my therapist recommended, which advised that I sit in front of my mirror at night and tell myself I was worthy and loved. She encouraged me draw: no joke my room was a mini studio by high school, and I loved it! She even encouraged me to run, but mostly when I had an attitude. It's funny how pent up emotions just melt away on runs.

She had a way of turning a negative situation into a positive outlook like it was an art. The thought process that goes into training yourself to be positive isn't easy, but she found ways of sprinkling in the good for me to see in every situation. This one time, I received a secret message from an anonymous person that said I was kind and pretty, and all these other good qualities, but then they followed it with my only flaw was I was conceited. I hated everything about myself at that point and so to be called conceited made me feel horrible because the people pleaser in me didn't understand what I did wrong. My mom pointed out that out of all the amazing things they said, I focused only on the one negative. She had me go back and read out loud all the great things they wrote to help me see the importance of focusing on the good. The more she helped me focus on the positive, on top of learning to like myself, the more my mindset slowly started to transform.

Like I said, ninja knowledge.

One of my favorite things she did to get me out of a funk was introduce me to music. After that rude message she introduced me to Little Richard, Marvin Gaye, and The Temptations. I was in LOVE. When she wasn't home, I'd blast them on the tape player and dance around the house. The living room was my stage and if that meant pushing all the furniture against the walls, so be it! I'm sure our neighbors loved me now that I remember we shared walls. But, I was a young kid discovering new music and had a lot of energy. The one band I'm sure she regretted showing me around that time was the Beach Boys. I could listen to them all day and I did! When we drove somewhere that is the CD I'd put on over and over until one day she calmly rolled down the window and threw it out.

I guess she had enough.

Where's the positivity in that mom?!

When she wasn't helping me build a strong mindset and discover new music, we would eat cheesecake and watch *Lifetime* movies together. As we watched stories like the young cheerleader being murdered by someone she bullied, another girl getting murdered for sleeping with another girl's boyfriend, and a love-drunk lady too blinded by her infatuation to see that she was walking into a death trap, my mom would have me take notes. During the commercial breaks she would have me point out all of the signs the girls missed that led them to their final tragic ends. She pointed out men's behavior and would ask me what I would do in situation type A compared to situation type B.

I honestly loved this and believe this is where my love for true crime came from. By watching those movies, I learned the world is a twisted and, while there are good people, you should always be on the lookout. What my mom did helped me see signs of abuse that weren't physical. She taught me that if I was going to be kidnapped there was a higher chance it would be by someone we knew. And that if I was ever to find myself in one of these situations, this is what to do;

Situation A:

Someone gets in your car and tells you to drive somewhere, or they'll shoot you.

Well, the first thing you are NEVER TO DO is drive them where they want you to because they're probably going to kill you anyway. And honestly what they have in mind is probably a lot worse than being shot. So instead, you make sure you're buckled in and crash your car into a close object. They most likely won't be wearing their seat belt and will go flying, but failing that, they can't take you to their location if you don't have a car.

Situation B:

You're walking home and your mom's friend drives by and rolls down the window. He or SHE offers you a ride. You think, of course, this is my mom's friend, why not.

Well, it's because they might want to kidnap you, or worse. Unless you call your mom confirming it is okay to get in that car, you do not take that ride. This one might be a bit strict, but my mom saw a lot of dark things and this one was the one she emphasized the most. We even had a password to know if the person was telling the truth after I tried to call her once and she didn't pick up. That idea came after one of Courtney's boyfriends picked me up from theater practice and no one had informed me of the change. I refused to get in his car and tried to call my mom. She didn't pick up, and even though I didn't feel comfortable riding with him, I noticed that my little niece was in the backseat and if I didn't get in the car she would be alone with him. So, I got in and thankfully he drove us home.

Shortly after that though, Courtney came to our mom and asked her to do a background check on him since she had a weird feeling when her and her boyfriend had sex. After looking up his history my mom discovered he was a sex offender. She broke down and apologized for putting Sana and myself in a situation where we couldn't protect ourselves if it called for it.

Luckily, we never had to use the passwords we created but after that experience our mom was a lot more protective.

She wanted to keep me safe, and I loved her for that. Although later, I learned it was not a normal thing for most girls to study *Lifetime* movies and to learn how to find sex offenders in their neighborhood. But hey, what about my childhood was "normal" at this point, am I right.

Thoughts On The Honeymoon Stage

This chapter brings a few things to mind. One being how much I wish I could go back and hug this small version of myself. I still don't understand how little me handled so much and it breaks my heart that she felt so alone. I want to tell her to show our mom the drawings and talk about the nightmares because she could help. But, I was afraid of something my little self couldn't understand and that breaks my heart. There is this song that keeps popping in my head as the soundtrack of this this chapter and that is 'Melancholy Kaleidoscope' from the band All Time Low. The song talks about being stuck in a melancholy place while trying to find a way out by focusing on the good. That was me. That was my little hurting heart. During this time, it felt like I was floundering, as my past was trying to suffocate me with sadness, and as I'm fighting for air I'm grabbing flowers between each gasp and telling myself life can be beautiful, and I'm safe and deserve this.

At the time I didn't know I was suffering with survivor's guilt and it was something therapy could have helped with, but you know the story on that. I do wish I would have talked in those sessions, because I didn't learn to identify this feeling until my early twenties. But I didn't, and the survivor's guilt would show itself after my visits with Robert when I would enter a stage of depression but refused to acknowledge it. Turns out that hiding my sadness was a trauma reaction and something I should have talked about with my therapist too. Whoops. I was also not as good at hiding my depressive episodes in private as I thought. Eventually my relapse of breakdowns would cause me to cut off communication with Robert.

There was a lot of pain to remember and rehash from this point in my life, but reading this chapter over while humming All Time Low,

I can't help but smile still. Out of so much emerging pain and uncertainty there was my mom guiding me and holding my hand, showing me a better way of life. Trusting her was my biggest challenge in the honeymoon stage because I didn't trust mother figures. I was always testing her and trying to prove that she would leave me like Lynn. I did this in ways that tested her anger and pushed her limits because I wanted to prove I was right, and she would give up on me. She never did though, and after one episode of tearing her down she told me that just because someone gives birth to you doesn't make them your mom. It takes actions and love and support to be a mother figure and that no matter how hard I pushed she wasn't leaving me. So, I pushed harder. And she kept providing methods of growth and words of affirmation, but most of all love.

Really though, my honeymoon stage was ugly. It was a stage of emotional scars and burns that were harder to hide with gel pens. Luckily, I had an amazing role model to help me focus my thoughts on the good and showed me that I can still turn those burns and scars into something beautiful so long as I focused on the good that surrounded me in life. The good was my imaginary gel pen flower petals and, with time, instead of them covering my knee or arm, they encompassed all of me like a protective aura.

So, I am pretty much a walking flower which is the coolest thing ever, including that I give some people allergies.

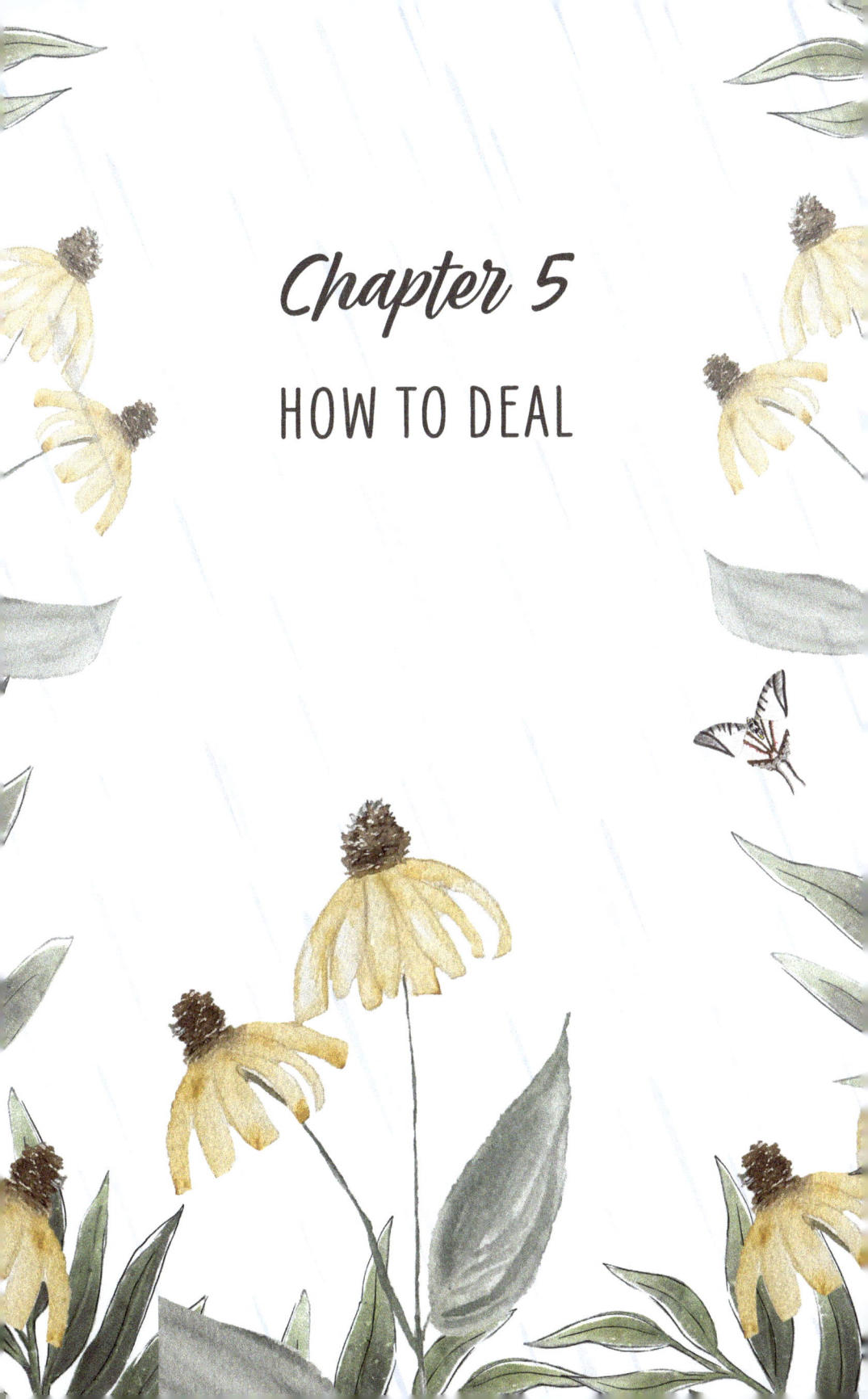

Chapter 5

HOW TO DEAL

5

My melancholy middle school days eventually came to an end and I joined the ranks of high schoolers. The summer before my freshmen year was one for the books and the best way to start a new chapter. My mom thought it would be a great idea for me to go on a summer mission trip with my youth group instead of locking myself in my room to sketch all summer. The car ride to Tennessee involved listening to Ellen DeGeneres on someone's iPod shuffle as she talked about finding baby spiders in shoes. My motion sickness brain could only handle so much Ellen and I napped most of the way up. That trip changed my life and taught me a couple of life lessons. One was to take the leap. I was the last one to go rappelling down the mountain because of my fear of heights and after pacing back and forth for what felt like hours, I somehow found the courage to do it. Maybe I was afraid of being the only one who chickened out. As I leaned back expecting to plummet to my death, my feet pushed against the wall of stone, my heart in my throat. Next thing I know I'm kicking off the wall and making my way slowly down. I remember holding on for dear life and praying the rope didn't break. I refused to look down but hey I did it and you guys, it was invigorating! I felt strong and pretty badass. It was so much fun that I didn't even question the height of the waterfall we jumped from a day later.

The second lesson learned on the trip was that although I can't see the Lord, he is with me. Sometimes I need a reminder on this one, not going to lie. Anyway, our group explored the nearby caves and we were eventually led into a cold and musky open area; above us hung giant mineral formations that looked like they were petrified as they dripped down. Our shadows were cast on the walls of the cave by our lights, which reflected on parts but didn't fully cover the whole chamber. We were asked to put one hand in front of our face and to turn off our lights. I stood there in a pitch-black cave knowing my hand was in front of me but not able to see even an outline of it. We were in pure blackness, and it was terrifying. Our youth pastor explained that in the same way that I couldn't see my hand, but knew it was there, God is present despite not appearing before our eyes. At first, I was afraid and wished the boy I had a crush on would grab my hand and we'd get married and have cute little Rockstar babies, but after he had his friend tell me I wasn't his type under the waterfall I am happy he didn't because that lesson would have been overshadowed. Plus, I'm almost positive that God has ADHD too and that's why while he is here with me, he might be focused on something else at the same time. Anyway, not only did I learn some life lessons, I discovered my love for Mother Nature. I can pinpoint this discovery to a particular moment. We were hiking up the mountain, and it had started to rain. So, we put our ponchos on and took a seat on the path while we waited for it to lighten up. As I sat there in my poncho, leaning on my backpack and watching the rain fall on everything around me, I felt calm. The mountain rain was powerful and almost had an echo to it, causing the trees and undergrowth to reverberate. It was a peaceful experience, and I knew I wanted more moments like that in my life moving forward. That trip left an incredible mark on me; it showed me that there was a feeling of calmness that existed in the world, and that I could find mine in nature.

When I returned home, things were changing in the house for the better. My mom turned down a position in Tallahassee, and she decided to adopt one of Courtney's foster sisters who was about to grow out of the system. Her name was Silver, and she was a Rockstar who had spikey hair and did flips and toe touches in skull pants. Courtney and Silver were complete opposites but on the same level of energy and quirkiness. Those two could keep a room laughing for hours to the point where your sides hurt. Once she moved in the three of us shared a bathroom and our wardrobes were pretty much a free for all. This caused a lot of fights that went from screaming to threatening because I would forget to return their clothes and often let friends borrow them. Our mom implemented a 48-hour rule and Terms and Conditions that we had to all agree on if were to continue to borrow clothes. You might be thinking: oh, that's just how sisters act. You're right, but keep in mind we are sisters from foster care. When Courtney and Silver fought, they really fought and as for me I kept my mouth shut and did sneaky little sister things like hide lizards in Courtney's pillowcases. For example, one weekend our mom was out of town for business and Courtney demanded I let her help me with my math homework. I informed her she was stupid and would mess it up and told her to go away. By time I had finished saying stupid Silver was standing in my doorway telling Courtney to leave it alone. Two seconds later Silver has Courtney in a headlock, and they are on the ground. The fight ended with Courtney's head being slammed into the wall, causing a hole. Within seconds the fight was over, and they were running to get the tools and paint to patch it up.

As for me, I looked at the hole silently, turned around and did my math homework.

Courtney and Silver had friends over all the time. Our mom had a rule where she had to meet all our friends. The friends Courtney and Silver brought home always had crazy colored spikey hair, and they all wore chains and baggy jeans with rock band t-shirts. Once she met them, they were good to hang out at the house so long as they were respectful of the rules. It wasn't uncommon to have them over for dinner or a holiday and our house always had people around. Trying to stay cool and hang with my older sisters and their friends, I started listening to the music they were into, which resulted in me reading a Slipknot song out loud in English class, talking about the poetic value of their verse.

Once Silver joined the picture, things sped up and other than remembering a few big moments the truth is I don't recall much of high school; it pretty much went by in a blur. I will say this, it was nothing like *She's All That* or *Jawbreaker* and for that I thank my lucky stars!

Halfway through my freshmen year Silver and Courtney moved out. Silver went to live with her birth family and Courtney got a place with some friends. It all happened so fast and out of nowhere. Silver wasn't going to tell us she was leaving and tried to move out in the middle of the night. I woke up to our mom and the girls in the front dining area and noticed there were suitcases by the front door. They were all talk-crying, and you could tell that emotions were tense. I just stood there in silence observing the scene. I had always heard of kids going back to their birth family after adoptions but never saw it first-hand. At one point Silver's friend came to pick her up and our mom asked them to come inside. They all sat at the dining room table and talked. Partly about showing respect and the proper way to handle certain situations, but mostly about it being okay that Silver wanted to go home. After that she drove off with her friend and I didn't see her again.

Not too long after that Courtney moved out with a few friends. The whole house changed when the girls moved out. It was quiet for the first time in a long time, and mine and my mom's days revolved around church, Costco adventures, and crime shows. Occasionally she would have a work event or dinner party at a friend's house that I could attend and that is where she would shine a light on me. She always introduced me as an amazing artist and called out how quickly I picked things up. This built my confidence because she explained exactly what it was that she liked, and I could repeat it to myself in the mirror during my nightly affirmation. The conversations at these events always ended up about kids in the system and behaviors they showed. One dinner party I overheard her say Courtney lived in a fantasy world and would continue to do so if she kept refusing her medication. Later that night I asked her about that and learned Courtney was bipolar and how people with bipolar can often stop taking their medication because they feel better, not realizing it was because of the medicine. I had no idea what that meant but knew that since she had moved out, she and mom argued more. To me her reasons for being hysterical or upset were understandable and our relationship stayed the same. This time was a nice period of my life. I loved the energy of the home when it was our mom and me, and I loved having an older sister who took on the world straight on but still came over to hang out with me.

Then, the summer going into my sophomore year, the universe said: that's enough quiet time little lady.

That summer my mom sent me away to stay with her best friend Jane and her husband Fred, who lived at the beach. Jane worked with my mom for years and was like an aunt to me. Her laugh could fill a room and she was all about girl power and bright colors. Fred was a neuropsychologist who studied PTSD. He was always curious to know my opinion on things and share his research with me. Spending the summer with them was one of the best summers and mini vacations. Every day involved Fred hooking me up to a machine and run breathing drills while reading and taking tests for a few hours. During free time Jane and I would hang out by the pool or go shopping. Being my mom's best friend, I was allowed to get away with more with her and she would talk my mom into letting me do things. On one shopping trip, Jane took me to get my makeup professionally done when at the time I wasn't allowed to wear anything but mascara and eyeliner. After that she took me to get a new swimsuit and I chose the one with ties on the side which Jane thought was super cute. Then we went and freshened up my hair. At this time my hair was beautiful and long, but I was feeling the Mandy Moore chop-off-all-hair type of rebellion and went pixie. By the end of the summer my mom picked me up wearing make-up, tie bikinis, and rocking a short crop. She wasn't too happy about the bikini but was okay with everything else and I was refreshed from a summer of being able to do nothing but relax.

When I returned home that summer Courtney had moved back home; she was pregnant and due in November. That was an experience and in the best way possible. Well... kinda. Courtney was back, but emotionally she was a different person. When she first arrived, she was sad and heavy from suffering a lot of hardship after moving out, but over time the excitement of becoming a mom shined through more. She would share details about the baby's size and what fruit it was compared to this time, she asked my opinion on baby clothes and let me help with setting up the crib. The experience was beautiful, and I couldn't wait to be an aunt. There was this little human living inside my sister's belly and to me it was the coolest thing ever. I couldn't wait to meet her. Our mom was over the moon too and was buying baby books galore and couldn't stop talking about the brain development of babies. Things were good, and we were all excited for our new friend.

The day Courtney went into labor I had just finished working the tech booth for a play when my mom's friend Rebecca pulled up, telling me to get into the car and that Courtney was at the hospital. Throwing all stranger danger warnings my mom ever taught me out the window, I hopped in that car. Rebecca drove to the hospital like we were going for a stroll in the park and when we finally arrived informed my mother that I was an aggressive back-seat driver for telling her to gun it through the yellow lights. No Rebecca, everyone knows the speed limit is 5 over the sign and that you don't break the moment the light turns yellow when you're already halfway through the intersection. It's not aggression, it's common sense. Or, it's the sheer panic that comes with trying to get to the hospital in time.

Really though, some things should not be ignored, and the rules of the road are one of them.

So, I'm brought back to a room where Courtney is pushing and people are surrounding her. I'm thrown a camera and jostled to the back of the room near the sinks with no idea what is happening. All that I am witnessing is the tip of a baby's head in between my sister's legs as she labors. Not sure what else to do I just keep clicking the camera out of fear and, I'm pretty sure, a sensory overload. My adrenaline and the chaos of the room combined to create a cacophony of noise around me. And then everything went silent. It was like the in the movie *Big Fish* where time stand stills and he moves through the popcorn. That is what happened but instead of popcorn in the air, the doctor was holding a weird alien baby up. She was beautiful.

Then seconds I was brought back to reality after watching the placenta placed on the medical table.

As it turns out that cute little alien baby was my new niece. Courtney brought Sana into the world November 14, 2005, and there to welcome her was her strong mom, an incredible grandma, the coolest aunt ever, and then Rebecca who stops mid-intersection at yellow traffic lights. Talk about a party!

When we finally were able to visit Sana, she was kicking and grabbing everything and I remember my mom looking over at me smiling ear to ear and saying, "We are going to have our hands full with this one." As I looked at the tiny alien baby, I couldn't help but smile either. It was instant love, and I was excited for a niece even if she did look like a raisin. She was my alien raisin.

Sana ended up being a sick baby and was in and out of the hospital a lot, suffering from colic in the beginning. I don't remember what she was in the hospital for, but one visit that stays in my head is when she was a bit older and standing in a playpen with other kids in the same room waiting for us to visit. She was wearing overalls and looked so sad. I don't know why that memory stuck but after that I tried to protect her the best I could. I had a fear of her dying after our friends lost their baby girl in a pool accident and as Sana got older, I tried to make sure she knew how to do certain things like go downstairs one step at a time or how to float if she fell in by mistake. It wasn't like that in the beginning but the anxiety of something happening to her grew over time. Don't get me wrong, I loved hanging out with Sana and showing her the world. We would listen to Baby Mozart together and I would take her on long walks in nature showing her leaves and grass. Talking about bugs and the sky. It was weird, I wanted to help her see the beauty in the world but at the same time I prepared her for the unpleasant and dangerous.

Before I knew it, Sana was almost three and I went from a sophomore to a senior in a blink of an eye. My mom had a heart attack that year and other than a few friend moments all I remember of my senior year is sitting in the hospital watching *Mamma Mia* with her and the feeling of uncertainty. When she was good to come home, Courtney moved out again, but Sana stayed with us. I'm not sure why but I knew she would also be moving out one day.

That same year I stopped eating and dropped down to 82 pounds. I'm 4'11" and graduated high school at 98 pounds which that is considered healthy so when I hit the 80 mark the whole family sat me down. I would eat only Cheerios throughout the day, grazing on a handful every now and then. Not because I was worried about my weight but because I wasn't hungry. I had lost my appetite. I snacked on Cheerios because they were small and they satisfied me.

Okay and maybe there's more to the story.

Ugh fine, I'll tell you!

Remember that ugly feeling I talked about earlier? This was me going through a stage of really hating my body and not understanding the importance of fueling it. Whenever I would look at food, I would feel nothing and would almost get disgusted by the look of it. As a result, I started to lose weight, a lot. Although I hated my body the truth was for the first time since losing weight when I looked in the mirror, I liked what I saw. My hip bones were showing when I wore low rise jeans and all my jean skirts hung off my waist. Women at church were complimenting me and noticing I had lost weight and it was a feeling I wanted more of. One of the girls I had gym class with was on track and she shared her workout routine with me which was going for a five-mile run before practice and another five-mile run after practice, but she was throwing up her food at night. I didn't like that idea and figured if I had lost weight from only eating Cheerios that I could continue to do that and pick up my workout routine. That was stupid. I couldn't even complete fences let alone a scrimmage on that amount of food, but I did it and put up with dizziness until someone forced me to talk about my issue.

The excuse of not being hungry didn't sit well with the adults. I had to start setting alarms for myself to remember to eat and even if my food tasted like sand I had to get it down. My mom, who was a frozen dinner queen, started to try more home cooked meals and we became fans of farmers markets and local produce shops. My weight picked back up and I was only allowed to work out on days I didn't have practice. A healthy balance and a great way to keep an eye on me.

Between my mom's heart attack and not eating the rest of the year faded and before I knew it prom and graduation happened.

Thoughts On How To Deal

When I look back at these years I think of my niece and the day she changed my life. Things changed drastically when she arrived, and I think she was always a part of Gods plan. The bond I had with her was my first real experience of understanding unconditional love. I didn't know it at the time. All I knew was I would do anything to protect her, and her happiness was my world.

Yes, I struggled with my mental health and body dysmorphia which totally needed to be addressed and luckily, I listened when it came to my body but even with all that going on, I was truly happy.

By the time high school had ended I had learned to focus my thoughts better and felt like I was a normal high schooler. I know that sounds like a ridiculous response but now that I'm older and watching high schoolers go through the same worries I had about not fitting in or feeling like an outcast I'm realizing we all felt that way. Watching my family go through so many changes with Silver moving out, Courtney moving out then back home pregnant to then leave again, on top of my mom having a heart attack and me dealing with my weight was normal to me. I think I felt calm although stressed because it was chaos. Instead of the chaos presenting itself in a foster care setting it presented itself in life events and I was sitting back sipping tea inviting it into my life. So much so that I felt safe and that dark shadow figure that I kept seeing at my door disappeared.

The last day I saw the shadow man was when Silver and Courtney were living at the home and I was in my room drawing. I looked up and saw him continuing to mock my existence even after all those years. I refused to let him win and called for Courtney and Silver to come into the room and look at him. When they arrived and I tried to show them the shadow, but he was gone. After that I didn't see him again. He just disappeared. To me that meant I was finally at a turning point for the better, or so I thought.

I was, however, not processing everything like I should have been doing and some traumatic experiences were pushed down but because I was so familiar with pushing them down I felt normal. For instance when I cut off all communication with Robert in my junior year. My breakdowns weren't getting better and by that point Robert was no longer in a behavioral home and was staying with fosters since he was about to grow out of the system. Fosters who wrote me emails explaining how it was my duty to take care of my brother and how I was selfish for ignoring his needs. One email that came in caused me to have a panic attack and my mom asked me if I wanted to continue contact. In the moment I said no, and she assured me it was okay, and I was allowed to change my mind. I never did but I never gave Robert a proper explanation on why I cut off communication. I didn't talk about it after that with anyone and instead said I was fine but then one evening ended up going for a run that resulted in me staying out all night without telling anyone where I was. The next day I woke up and was sitting in an orange grove and knew I had messed up. I was too afraid to call my mom of course and knew I couldn't just walk through the front door and say sorry about that, so instead called my youth pastor. One of the older girls came and picked me up and took me out to lunch where we talked. She gave me a book called *Redeeming Love* and told me to hold on to it and read it when the time was right, then took me home. As it turned out the church was aware of my disappearance. My mom had reached out to see if I ran to youth group by chance when I didn't come home. Trust me, I would have gone to youth group instead, but somewhere along my run my legs took me to an orange field and my mind lost track of time.

I wasn't in trouble when I came home and instead was greeted with an overwhelming hug from my mom. At one point in the night officers asked her if I had any identifying body marks and she broke down. Courtney had to step in and tell them about my birth mark on my stomach but then decided to also tell them about my secret tattoo. A stupid home tattoo my friend made on me with a needle one day after school. After all the hugging was over and everyone was happy to know I wasn't dead my mom asked me to show her, and of course she grounded me for that.

So yeah, while I was happy and feeling as comfortable as a teenage girl could. I was turning off at points and continued to ignore signs that showed I needed additional help. Totally normal!

6

This chapter had many different introductions and that's because I hate this next part.

I thought about starting it with my safe zone because personally this chapter makes me uncomfortable, and I am trying to tell my anxiety brain I am safe and it's okay and to continue to write the darn story.

That introduction went like this;

'I love the ocean. My favorite times to be at the beach are during a storm, king tide, or at night. During those times it's not that crowded and more times than not I'm by myself. The ocean to me is like sitting on those mountains during a rainstorm in my poncho. The ocean, just like the rain, knows how to calm my soul. After high school it went from being the site of partying and causing a ruckus into my place to think. A place that helped me calm my nerves when all I wanted to do was disappear and start a new life. I could tell my secrets to the waves, and so I did.'

Then I realized...

I don't know how to transition from that; and thought, Girl stop being so deep and just tell the story.

So, then I thought about saying it straight, which went like this;

I loved my life and the direction it was going after high school, then the world took my mom, and I went numb.

Too dark?

The thing is, after high school I took time off before going to college and loved it. My mom knew I was afraid of college, so she didn't pressure me too much but did encourage me to start looking after a year. With Courtney gone that meant me stepping in and helping with Sana. I would drive her to her early education program and pick her up. When she came home, we played games, went swimming, and took walks. Watching her grow and learn her colors was my form of entertainment. We were inseparable; I started helping in the children's nursery at church just to hang out with her. Anywhere we went together was turned into an adventure and she was my little best friend. The memory of her I will always cherish is when she was around three or four. I'd be awake but not fully, lying in bed dozing and I would hear her little footsteps outside in the hall. She would knock quietly on my door before cracking it open and tip toeing towards my bed. As she slid under the covers, I would act asleep and start snoring obnoxiously. She would giggle and close her eyes to pretend she was sleeping too and make little snoring sounds. It's one of my favorite memories of her and it reminds me of sunshine and warmth.

Sana lived with my mom and me for a year before Courtney came back for her. When Courtney returned, she was talking about growing up in Texas and how horrible her life was, which I found grating, knowing all of it wasn't true. Our mom tried to talk Courtney into allowing Sana to transition to the new place slowly since she hadn't lived with Courtney for a year. That wasn't what Courtney wanted to hear, so she accused our mom of keeping her child from her. Then she picked up Sana with no consideration of how it would impact her, using the excuse that she was her child.

My mom would visit her constantly and would come home and cry at the state of Courtney. She did her best to continue to make sure Sana experienced childhood joys like holidays and family trips, but she couldn't control what happened in Courtney's home. When Easter came around my mom called Courtney to wish them a Happy Easter and Sana said the Easter Bunny didn't come by. My mom instantly grabbed her chest and tried to hold back tears. I witnessed her heart break as she held a stable tone and said, "Do you know what that silly bunny did? He thought you still lived here and dropped off your gifts at my place! Isn't he just silly?" When the call ended, she broke down and could barely speak.

Soon after that Sana came over and found all the gifts the silly Easter Bunny had left.

Around the same time my mom's personality started to change. She would say things that didn't make sense or mean things that were out of character before forgetting about it. At the time I thought it was best for me to move out too, not realizing personality change can occur in patients who have had strokes. Now I know that doctors believed my mom had mini ones before her heart attack. Looking back, I can tell moving out crushed her horribly and I wish I could change that. At the time I thought she was mad at me for being there which is silly looking back at it, but I felt like she only wanted to be with Courtney and Sana, and it would be easier if I moved out.

I moved in with three local wake skaters down the road. It was great, I'm not going to lie. I loved those boys. Still do. They were all in school, but at the time I had not considered going back. Instead I planned to snorkel Florida Springs from the top of the state to the bottom.

Proud of my new place, I invited my mom to visit. I was excited to have her over and show her our home. I showed her my shoebox of a room and the wall the boys and I would climb and jump off into a gigantic bean bag. When she saw the mini half pipe in the garage, the insane amount of liquor in the kitchen, and one half-naked guy walking around the house, she dragged me home before I knew what was happening.

The great thing about being home was I was able to get back into a running routine that I had lost after moving out. I didn't know the roads well enough at my new place and didn't feel comfortable running by myself near the main road, so I stopped completely. After moving back home I picked it back up and when I tell you my body missed it, holy crap my first run was rejuvenating. Despite this positive change, I quickly became bored. I would still go out with friends but knew that I needed more. One afternoon I found myself in my mom's room talking about my snorkel plans and how I wanted to start the trip. After going on for about fifteen minutes she responded with, "You're never going to go to college."

First, how dare her! After I informed her how wrong she was, she responded with, "Prove it."

Excuse me?

Did she not learn anything from the smoothie situation?

She obviously did and that was how she knew exactly what she was doing when she said that, and her plan worked.

Shortly after that I signed up for community college and started taking classes. My schedule was mostly math and general education courses, but my last two classes of the day were sculpting and photography. The smell of dark room chemicals and spinning wheels just isn't something you get every day! I felt at home and got into that messy bun and lost-to-the-world zone when I took those classes. The small classroom setting felt comfortable to me, and I was a bit sad I hadn't started earlier. I had no idea what college really offered until I experienced it myself. I could see why my mom wanted me to go. You see college isn't just a piece of paper. In fact, it's more than that. It teaches you self-discovery, opens opportunities, and challenges you tap into your problem-solving skills. If that isn't enough, think of all the cool clubs you can join like chess or swing dancing! I highly recommend it for anyone who is on the fence.

When my first semester had ended, I realized I still had no idea what I wanted to do. I could see myself doing so many things and sadly *National Geographic* had still not reached out begging for me to work for them. So, I turned to my mom, who wanted me to be an artist for anatomy textbooks. Random, I know!

It's not though, you see I love the human body, specifically the naked human body. So much so that my mom bought me my first art piece of a naked woman from an art show that I fell in love with at the age of twelve. So, an artist for anatomy books seemed like something up my alley. How I would get there, we both had no idea and looked at things like Art Teacher until somehow, we landed on Psychology. It looked like a well-rounded program that would keep my interest and I could build off. Plus, with this program I could see if I had any personality disorders like being a psychopath, which was a fear of mine. Not knowing my background scared me and let's just say I am a bit of a hypochondriac and think I have everything wrong with me. Getting a degree in Psychology would help me notice if I had any traits to be on the lookout for, and I could self-diagnose myself. So, it was perfect... right?

Starting college made my mom immensely proud but it annoyed Courtney. She resented the path I had taken, and accused me of acting perfect and said I was no better than her. Sadly, our relationship turned to mostly fighting. The sister I once admired and looked up to had started to become someone who annoyed me to the point that I would avoid her if possible. The hardest part of our relationship was keeping my mouth shut about her behavior. Every time my mom and I did anything Courtney didn't approve of she would threaten to not let us visit Sana.

When I say this made me angry, I can't even begin to describe the loathing that grew in me. I had to watch my sister walk all over my mom and then had to try and act like everything was okay. I couldn't do it. I refused to be a part of it and moved out again but this time in a more sensible place with a friend.

My mom didn't come to visit this time and I knew she was worried about me moving out – especially without sitting down and talking to her first. The events leading up to leaving happened quickly after having lunch with my friends and explaining I couldn't do it anymore and would end up saying something I regretted if I had to watch the situation with my mom and sister play out. At the time I thought she didn't approve of me moving out but looking back I can tell she was thrown off from my rushed decision-making and my actions added to her hurt. During that time, though, I was jealous of the attention

Courtney received for her actions and felt like no matter how hard I tried to do the right thing it wasn't enough. At the time, I felt ignored and rejected by this – although I was reaching out for more independence, I still wanted to feel I had their attention and love. It was a vulnerable time for me, with lots of change, which exacerbated those feelings, and maybe closed off a multifaceted view of the situation.

When I would go home to visit our conversations were always about Courtney and her new boyfriend and his family. They didn't like us from the stories Courtney told them about us, and our mom knew they spoke poorly of us when we left. She ignored it and said let them think what they want, but I couldn't. They were attacking her character based off lies and all I wanted to do was tell them they were wrong and tell Courtney to stop being a manipulating bitch.

Every holiday we would meet at our mom's place, but this year Courtney wanted to have Christmas at her house. At this time Courtney was living in a trailer that was infested with bugs and I didn't want to sleep on the floor. I told her I'd show up early morning before they opened gifts. She was insulted and told me to not show up at all and once again accused me of being superior. When I didn't show up, she told our mom she was joking, and I shouldn't be so sensitive. By this time, I was used to our mom taking Courtney's side because of her cruel way of dangling Sana in front of us and knew I had no argument and didn't try to defend myself. I would ignore the calls from my mom because I didn't want to talk about it. I felt it was unfair how she always took her Courtney's side and was annoyed I would be the one to have to apologize.

New Years went by, and I had still not reached out. My second semester started, and I was consumed by classes and then a few weeks into school I had a nightmare that scared me. I'm someone who remembers my dreams very vividly and sometimes it bites me in the butt. This one was one of them.

THE NIGHTMARE

My roommate and I were showing our families our new castle and were about to start a tour up the stairs when a loud and thunderous knock came from the front door. A strong gust of wind howled throughout the house, whistling through the gaps, and the lights flickered. The banging became louder and my roommate and I were scrambling to get the parents out of there to somewhere safe. When I grabbed my mom, she was in a black gown. I grabbed her arms as the banging got closer and told her I would be okay, and that she could go.

Then I woke up.

That was Monday and that Tuesday in English we were covering a poem between a mother and a daughter that spoke about forgiveness. When I heard the poem, it reminded me to forgive, and I made a doodle note to call my mom and then decorated the word forgiveness in flowers. After class that day I went home to find a Facebook message on my laptop.

The Facebook message read, "Patricia, where are you? Have you spoken to your sister? We need to talk to you." It was my mom's best friend Jane. She informed me everyone had been trying to reach me for a few hours. Not thinking it was a big deal I asked her if everything was okay.

"Your mom passed. Patricia I'm so sorry. Where are you?"

I froze after reading her response. It didn't make sense. The words felt fake, almost like a sick prank. I didn't understand what was happening, so I walked trying to comprehend what the world had just told me. I walked until I found myself at my boyfriend Craig's parents' house. They instantly knew something was wrong, but I couldn't find the words to let them know. I kept trying to tell them, but the words didn't come out and my mind couldn't connect the dots. When I was finally able to get the words out, they made everything speed up but freeze at the same time.

"My mom, she's dead."

Soon after, I found myself in the backseat of a car. My roommate and Craig were in the front, and I had been given a jacket and shoes. They were taking me to my mom's house. When we arrived, there were so many people in uniforms standing around and going inside and outside of the house. My sister was the first to come over as we walked up. She knew I didn't want to be touched and pulled me away from everyone trying to hug me. I was thankful for her in that moment but felt helpless when they brought out our moms' body bag and others had to hold back Courtney as she screamed. She screamed and I stood there frozen just watching. I watched as the world around me moved in slow motion and all the sound disappeared.

I had no thoughts because to me it wasn't real. That was my house and that was my mom. If this was real, then what did that mean?

I didn't know how to process it and the person who had helped me understand my emotions was gone and I couldn't comprehend that.

The days following were a blur and lead to a few events that left a lot of questions. The night after they had taken our mom away, our family home had been broken into and destroyed. The person busted through my bedroom window and took a bunch of documents and files. I had lived there for eleven years with no disturbance, so it didn't make sense for the break in to happen just then. It didn't take long for one of our moms' friends to reach out and let us know that Courtney called him late that night asking him to fix a window, which he had refused.

The night my uncles got into town they took over the funeral planning. They decided our mom would be buried with their parents in North Carolina and we would have her funeral there as well. As they planned that, our mom's friends the Mixers planned a celebration of life gathering at their house for local friends. My foster mom was there and found me hiding in a separate room. She sat next to me; this time I cried on her shoulder and instead of rocking me she hugged me tighter than ever and said it would be okay.

Talk about full circle.

During this time Courtney started asking a lot of questions about our mom's things and had no interest in coming around unless it involved her getting something. The night after our house was broken into my uncles and I searched through the house looking for mom's will. For some reason she didn't have a digital copy and we hoped it would be in the safe. The only problem was the safe was taken in the break in, so we crossed our fingers and started searching through all the remaining documents hoping to find something. Courtney didn't show up to help but made sure to let us know the paper should say "Last Will and Testament." This wouldn't come off as odd for many people but coming from Courtney, it didn't make sense for her to know the details of what the will would look like. After many hours of searching, we decided it would be best to divide things up between the family. The next day we all met at our mom's house and started distributing things. Courtney called the paintings, china, bed, kitchen silverware, and pretty much anything she could. I didn't want anything but was told I needed to take something because later on I would regret it. I ended up with a section of my grandma's wedding china, a dinner ring and twist watch that belonged to my mom's grandparents. When it came to decide who took the car, my mom's friends and my uncles encouraged me to take it, since I didn't have one. Courtney demanded that she deserved it since she had a family, and I would like the TV. I didn't care to fight her and said okay. Courtney handed me the TV and continued to pack our mom's car and her car with boxes. She had to have a friend come over to drive one car back to her place. Later that night she posted a picture of her having a huge bonfire getting rid of useless documents and a few weeks later sold the car.

Before heading to North Carolina for the funeral, the mortician offered us to chance to see our mom. Courtney couldn't do it and that's okay. A lot of people told me not to do it, but I had to. I had to see that she was truly gone because if I didn't see it, I believed that meant she was tired of me and packed up and moved away. That was my past trauma coming back to the surface. I trusted my mom and knew she would never leave like that but of course my brain went there instantly when she passed. Maybe it was trying to make sense of the situation with something I was familiar with. Nothing changed after seeing her body though, other than the fact that I knew she didn't abandon me. That image of her didn't stay in my mind like people warned. She looked like she was sleeping and what stayed with me was the assurance that I wasn't left again. I cried, because I wanted to hug my mom and because she was really gone. I would never be able to hug her again.

Her funeral in North Carolina was beautiful and I knew she was there in spirit when the others told stories of her. Watching my family laughing at the immense joy she brought to this small part of the world made the pain easier that day. It wasn't until my flight back to Orlando that I felt truly alone, and my thoughts turned. I didn't understand how family worked outside my mom. She was the one always planning trips and staying connected with everyone. I had no idea how to do that. She was my central point, and now suddenly I was out of orbit, spinning wildly through blank space. All I could think was, am I still a part of the family now that the funeral was over, or did my adoption end when she was gone? As the thoughts filled my head, I put my headphones in and cried during take-off, not knowing what to do next.

Thoughts On Growing Pains

Barf.

I'm joking!

But like, not really. That was hard.

The day I stood in my mom's room talking about my snorkeling trip is one memory that has stuck. It was late morning, but she was dressed and looked like she was heading out soon. I was bored, in a rut, and wanted to tell her about my plans. The whole time I went on about my trip she was silent. I knew she was analyzing me, but I still had no idea what she was thinking. If you are in therapy, you'll know the feeling. It's when you tell your therapist something and instead of replying or acknowledging you, they do the worst thing ever which is write something down and look right back at you.

Maybe it's a reminder to pick up ham on the way from work but in my mind it's *oh great I'm a psychopath*.

That was a look I was all too familiar with by this time in my life.

I could always tell when my mom was just going with the flow and when she was processing how to handle a situation. Picking up body language and emotions came naturally to me.

When she interrupted my spiel, I expected it and wasn't thrown off. She had finally figured out how to approach the situation but what she actually said was not what I was expecting.

Touché mother dear, touché.

This memory makes me smile, for one because I can still see her face and her sitting on her bed with her legs crossed. The clear memory of her expression at the time fills me with love for her.

College to me was scary at first because outside of partying I didn't understand what it was, and it confused me. It wasn't required but at the same time it was expected but then at the same time not everyone could make it or afford it. But again, it was expected. Confusing right?

I kept hearing: you will be the first to go to college from your birth family, and that was terrifying. College was the norm in my family and to hear I would be the first from "my birth family" made me question if I was good enough to do it. I hate that I was told that. I know it's meant to be something to be celebrated but I hated it. If my birth family hadn't done it, then could I? I mean I know I was adopted but maybe nature over nurture was inevitable!

That is obviously not true. But that's my anxiety heart for you, and it's something that I think many adopted kids will at least think about, if not struggle with.

By this time, I understood my trauma for the most part and by understood, I mean I knew not to focus on it. My brain favored positivity over negativity, so I was suppressing anything negative like a pro. I didn't even have to try anymore. My brain's pathways created an express lane for those negative and traumatic experiences. As for anxiety, that made sure to shine through no matter how hard the pathways pushed it away.

When I finally did go to college, I realized my anxiety had betrayed me, and I had been missing out. Once I discovered the hidden treasures of higher education I never wanted to leave. I would still go back and take classes if I could afford to be a professional student. The idea that so much knowledge was in one spot blew my mind and I felt like I was discovering who I was. It was a beautiful time in my life, and I miss it. Not the feeling of enjoying college but the feeling of self-discovery during a time when I felt the happiest and had the support of my biggest cheerleader.

When I lost her, it started to feel like I was on an unbalanced spinning wheel that was rocking out of control. I felt like I was forced to grow up and had no idea how to do it. Before her funeral I had no true responsibilities and was still calling my mom to set up doctor appointments. I was a child and looking back at this reminds me of that. During this time, I felt stupid for not understanding how to plan a funeral, what a Last Will and Testament looked like, or what the next steps were after a parent died. I was hard on myself and angry for being so naïve and unaware. I'm sorry for treating my twenty-one-year-old self that way. It wasn't until my thirties that I realized I shouldn't have been so mean to myself because twenty-one, no matter how old it may sound at the time, is still a baby. The human brain hasn't even finished developing yet! That was the time I was supposed to start becoming best friends with my mom, and when our relationship would enter a new stage – an experience I miss more than ever and one that didn't get any easier over the years as I grew up. If anything, it only became harder because I saw those around me have that relationship with their parents. I wanted that connection with my mom. Before that stupid fight we were almost there. Yeah, we fought but never I wanted her to leave forever and when it was her time, I felt it was my fault.

That dream did not do me justice and in fact hurt me more. After the funeral I couldn't stop thinking of the dream and I felt like if I had told my mom that I needed her to stay she wouldn't be gone. I felt like I gave her permission and I hated myself for that. I hated myself for fighting with her over something so stupid and I hated myself for not knowing what to do next.

So, like I said before, barf.

This chapter was hard to acknowledge because there wasn't a lot to focus on that was positive and that's okay. I've come to realize it's okay to be sad and it's okay to not find the positivity in everything. Sometimes a situation can simply suck.

And that is this whole experience.

Death is an experience everyone goes through and it's one that can't be covered up with gel pen flowers. Instead, it requires nurturing and watering those flowers to help keep them strong.

Chapter 7

GOOD GRIEF

7

Death sucks lets be real, and the thing that got me most was death didn't just happen and go away. It filled my nightmares to the point where I had to stay with a friend and her mom because I couldn't sleep without dreaming of demons dragging me to hell or watching the people I loved being eaten by whatever creature my brain came up with. It put a fog over my perception, my senses were dulled, and the idea of moving on physically hurt. Right when I decided I was able to move forward and go back to my daily life, a sharp pain pierced my heart and I had a breakdown in the dairy cooler while out grocery shopping. I crawled back into bed. Watching everyone go back to their own lives felt wrong to me when all I wanted to do was scream. Eventually I would have to go back and when the smell of rye bread made me cry, I knew I could cry to myself in the bathroom, wash my face and then get back to slicing bread.

After the funeral and everything went back to normal, I found myself back at our mom's house cleaning up. The place was in disarray from dividing things up and there were objects still lying around that needed to be packed away. Courtney was living out in country so I knew I should do it. There were clothes in the closet and in our mom's drawers, so I started with them. I don't know why but I tried to be gentle with them, taking my time to fold each shirt and making sure it wasn't wrinkled. As for her jeans I was sure to fold them like she had before putting them in a trash bag.

Cleaning up was harder than I thought, and before I knew it, I was looking at the bottom of a toilet bowl throwing up for no reason. When nothing else came up I leaned against the wall and stared at her shower. Her shampoo and body wash were still there like she could home at any moment and take a shower and all this was just a part of a horrible dream. That thought immediately sparked more vomit.

After pulling myself together and packing up the remaining clothes, I took them to Goodwill. I decided to keep one shirt of hers. It was one her favorites that looked like a sweater over a collared v neck shirt and it still smelt like her. I kept that shirt wrapped in a bag in a box in my closet and would take it down occasionally to hold. That went on for about three years when one day I went to smell it and her smell was gone. So, I did the normal thing and put it back, but this time forgot until I was packing one day and saw it. I smiled and folded it and then put it in a Goodwill bag and dropped it off. Did I regret that a few months later? Yup, but it was a moment of growth that needed to happen.

After her death my behavior became reckless. I returned to school, which was a stupid decision. Except that, I was wrapped in a bubble of grief that made it seem like I wasn't making choices, just sleepwalking through life. I should have taken time off but instead went and sat in classes and took tests on subjects I had no idea about. I was going through the motions of my daily life, but it was like my body was in auto pilot and everything else was numb. In my mind I told myself it was okay to skip a final and go rock climbing because I could retake the course. I was making excuses for myself, and it got to the point that I lost my scholarships and financial aid. I was ashamed and so to cover the fact that I was struggling to pay for classes on my own, I told everyone that I had dropped to part-time study in order to work and save at the same time. I couldn't risk seeing my own failure reflected back at me in their expressions. I had worked extremely hard to get there and to lose it all meant failure; that was a reality I found difficult to face. I was barely a halftime student and took maybe one course once a semester because that was all I could afford out of pocket. Losing my scholarships was a bit of an eye opener but I honestly didn't care. I knew the consequences and brushed them off. At this point in my life, I felt nothing. To me the world was a dream, one that I couldn't wake up from.

There was one moment that happened during this time that did give me some sort of peace. One day I was sitting on a bench outside after failing another test and I remember thinking: *what's the point.* That was when an old friend from high school sat down next to me. He didn't say anything for about five minutes and just sat there observing his Vans. Then he spoke. He gently said he was sorry about my mom and then, after a pause, said it would all be okay, that it gets easier. I didn't say anything, I just smiled at him in response. He got up and walked away and I never saw him again. I'm pretty sure he became a park ranger somewhere in Oregon, but I won't ever forget how his small act of kindness made me feel then. Mostly because it was like he knew I needed to hear that especially in that moment. I'm not sure if Eric lost someone but the way he said he was sorry felt like he understood and that's what I appreciated.

I needed to know I wasn't alone. I knew others were also hurting but my brain only reminded me of my pain. Death is a part of life, and we know to expect it, but it has a dark magic over it that shields the eyes from seeing that others are hurting too because all its presenting to you is your own darkness. It truly sucks. Before Eric approached me that day I had heard "I'm sorry about your mom", repeatedly and I know everyone was being genuine and meant it, but I felt like they didn't get it. There would be times when I would want to talk about my mom with friends but they would change the topic or offer to go out partying to cheer me up. Her death anniversary went from me wanting to visit her and family to partying at the Gasparilla Pirate Festival where we let a balloon go that had a message to her. It ended up being a trip that I went to every year for a while, and I looked forward to it, but it was also a trip that brought out a lot of emotion. Combined with alcohol, it would often result in me breaking down when I returned home because I felt like no one understood what I was going through. Although my friends were trying to cheer me up, I felt disconnected. I knew visiting family would mean facing emotions I wasn't strong enough to let the light shine on, so I ignored my true needs and acted against what I wanted, allowing my plans to easily get derailed. This only added to my emotional numbness, despair and not feeling like I had agency over myself.

Eric wasn't wrong, it would be okay, but not for a bit.

Around the same time our home was locked up and the state took it over. My mother was one of the thousands affected by the market crashing in 2008 and owed money on the house. Once that happened, there was no more going to just sit inside or clean. I would go on Google Maps and type in our address just to see our mom's car sitting in the driveway. I know that's creepy, but they did it in *Men in Black* and I thought it was good way to remember the home I missed. At least, it was one of the only tangible ways that I could at the time. If you can't tell already, my behavior started to down spiral around this time. I found myself pushing everyone away. I broke up with my boyfriend Craig and started distancing myself from old friends. This, my friend, is where the self-sabotage comes in, a beautiful trait I have inherited from my previous trauma. What was different about it this time was I didn't try and argue with what I was doing and correct it like I had learned to do over the years. I was purposely not going into work and starting arguments for no reason. My behaviors added up and the warnings continued until they let me go. The day that happened it was pouring as I rushed to my car and before I could leave the parking lot I broke down. Thankfully the rain was a Florida Summer thunderstorm, and no one could see inside the windows without getting too close. I had lost the job I had for seven years and was suddenly jobless and broke with no backup. I couldn't run home to my mom and ask for help. I screwed up, and what made it worse was I knew they were right. I wasn't okay and was becoming unreliable and untrustworthy. I couldn't admit it to my roommate that I was fired and told them I quit. They looked at me like I was insane, which they had every right to. I laughed about it but inside I was really freaking out. They didn't get the joke, and neither did I. I was in extreme panic mode. At the time I had a friend who worked as a shot girl for a night club and she introduced me to her manager. He gave me a job. At first I was excited because I would be the shot girl who walked around getting paid to have fun. My outfit consisted of heels, booty shorts, a corset, and tights. I felt sexy and loved it. As it turns out I only liked it when I was in my bedroom and by myself. When it came to me working on the club floor, let solo after the first few nights of training, the ugly side of people soon showed. People saw my body as an object to grab and pull in any direction they wanted. Whether it was placing their hands on my hips to lower me to their laps or resting their hand on my butt while ordering a drink. My body was nothing more than a grabbable shot table and I hated it but stayed. I needed the job, the money wasn't great and even though I hated being grabbed, I was telling myself I was having fun. I eventually found myself at a crappy little tattoo shop in a crappy little town getting a tattoo that covered the top right of my arm. So cliché, I know. Can I be any more of a *Lifetime* movie?!

Ugh, anyway.

It wasn't until I looked in the mirror and saw what I had done that it was like I snapped back to myself. For the first time in a year and a half, I saw clearly. That moment felt like a fog finally lifted, and when it did, I was staring at huge tree branch covering my arm with a hummingbird around it, and my sad, drawn face looking back at me. My first thought was, *my mom would be so disappointed in me*. After thanking the guy, I drove two hours home, crying the whole way. What the hell had I just done? One evening I was talking to an older man at the bar while we were setting up for the night crowd when he looked at the bartender and told me to never get a tattoo like hers. That it was a way that woman devalued themselves. The bartender was going to school for law and was one of the strongest and smartest women I've ever met. He judged her on her tattoos and not who she was as a person and I remember thinking how wrong he was. I looked up to her and wanted to be that strong. At the time I thought I could get there with starting with a tattoo. Shortly after realizing the position I had put myself in with work and now a permanent tattoo, I freaked out and instead of being professional and quitting, I just stopped showing up for shifts all together.

Not cool, I know! I'm sorry!

After walking away from being a shot girl I found myself working two jobs that barely made rent. One was a night shift as a photo lab assistant at the drug store and the other was a food server at a local restaurant. That eventually turned into one job when schedules inevitably collided, and I couldn't make a mandatory meeting at the restaurant because I had a shift in the photo lab. My pay checks paid for a pound of turkey and chocolate milk, a summer class, rent, and bar hopping. That was, until a few months of working one job that barely paid minimum wage meant that I fell behind on rent, leading me to selling my car to a local dealer. I didn't even get $500 for it, and the person who helped me sell it took the money and disappeared.

I was too stupid to see it coming, and by stupid, I mean too vulnerable.

That led to a breakdown because I was stuck unless I asked for help and that terrified me. I would have rather pulled my teeth and sold them on the black market than ask for help but obviously that wasn't an option.

Also, like how do you even find the black market?

Asking for a friend...

I ended up calling a cousin of mine. He was someone I trusted and had built a unique bond with over the years. When I called him asking for help, he asked me what had put me there and I had to tell him. He wasn't angry, instead he was gentle. He reminded me a lot of how my mother would have approached the situation, and that was to look at the lesson presented and what I have learned and can change. I needed that talk, and he did help me out but made it clear I needed to get my act together. After our call, I cleaned up my resume and started applying for better paying jobs. Luckily my resume was basic level impressive for a simple receptionist position because of my mom. She created my resume in middle school after I typed up old work files as a punishment for lying. By senior year I had "worked" as a file assistant, cashier, event volunteer, and felt confident enough to apply to *National Geographic* one afternoon in the high school library. My mom also taught me to always be prepared and have a good resume on hand at any time. Mine would be in my email and thankfully that tip came in handy while attending a paint party with a girl from work. While we were pregaming in the parking lot one of the girls mentioned she was leaving her job and moving to New Jersey and that her company was hiring.

    Trying to control myself and not look desperate I asked her if she could send me the link to apply. Instead, she told me to send her my resume and she'll look it over and give it to her boss. Before she could forget I searched through my emails like a mad woman and within seconds she had it emailed to her phone.

    That Monday, I received a call while eating a well-made burrito and did an introduction interview over the phone. Another golden lesson taught by mom, was that you never say it isn't a good time and ask to call back when a job offer is on the table. If you wanted the job you took the call and that is what I did. After it was over, I had a second interview date set up and a burrito waiting for my love, so I felt hopeful.

    The second interview ended with me talking about cat cafes and air filters and I was pretty sure I didn't get the job but a week later they called me back for a third interview. The only issue was, I was leaving for a beach camping trip the same day. At this point I knew if I didn't get this job I would be packing up and moving to North Carolina to live with my mom's best friend Jane. I put on my best interview outfit and wore my hair down to hide the bikini I was wearing underneath and had a solo interview with the director who said they'd be in touch. I left feeling good and was certain I had it. After a month of not hearing from them I had started packing my things and prepared to make the call and take my aunts offer. I was in the kitchen the day they called back and when they offered me the position, I had to ask them to repeat themselves. I was so set on them saying they found another person that I didn't understand when they asked if I wanted to be a part of their team.

Sweet baby Jesus...

I had done it.

I had somehow got a job working at a private university answering phones.

What just happened?!

I still remember the lighting of the room that day, the way the kitchen window looked over the pond and the quietness of the home. I was by myself crying and holding the phone just saying thank you to myself on repeat. I can't tell you what I was doing before that but the moment I saw them calling my heart dropped and when the call ended it had determined my path. I would remain in Florida. Asheville would have been a beautiful place to live and it's one of my favorite places but my heart sings for salt water and summer nights. If only Asheville had an ocean view.

A month into the new job I had made two good friends from orientation, and we hit it off. Dan was a large hockey-loving Canadian who wore band sweatshirts and beanies and could have a conversation with anyone. He loved all things horror and knew the Horror Film History of Old Florida better than anyone I knew. Then there was Shannon, a girl who told her mom she was heading for college the same day she left. She was in the driveway packing up her suitcase when she told her mom she was heading to college. Like, what? I knew she was a badass from that moment. Dan and Shannon were what I needed, which was realness. For the first time since losing my mom I felt hopeful and that I was finally getting back on track, even if I was still lying about school and didn't have $50 in my bank account after rent. I felt good and excited for the future.

However.

The same time I was spiraling down, so was Courtney, but I couldn't see it. She would drop Sana off for the weekend and leave, every time looking thinner and thinner. I didn't notice she was suffering because I was trying to cover up my own pain and carefully put on the image of being okay every day. The only thing that had my concern during those interactions was to make sure Sana had a good visit. When she came over that was where all my attention went. I did everything in my power to make sure I had enough money to put food in the fridge and help give her good childhood moments. We'd dance and make music together or paint rocks and sticks we found on walks. I was very fortune to have friends who knew her and helped. We were able to get wrist bands to the local museums where we'd learn about dinosaurs and space, and I was able to take her kayaking in the local lakes thanks to my roommate's family. Courtney and I were both loved by one of the most incredible souls who would do anything for us and what she provided and created for us was beautiful. I wanted that back and wasn't ready to let that go. When Sana came over, I wanted to help make her memories as joyful as possible, because she deserved it. She was a child who lost a grandmother and was going through unstable times at home, and when she visited, I tried to give her what I knew and loved. I wish I was in a better mindset at the time because then maybe I would have seen the signs from Courtney earlier on, but I wasn't. When I did finally realize where she was mentally, I didn't know how to bring her back. She had moved out, left her husband with the kids and was staying with random men.

Almost a year went by without her reaching out and the day she did she started asking for money. She was still living with random men and couldn't have weighed more than 100 pounds. There was a rumor going around that she was doing heavy drugs but when I asked about it, she denied it. I didn't want to give her money and I offered to buy groceries. When groceries didn't work, I offered to buy a pizza and have her pick it up at a place near her. Every call was always something more and another reason for needing money. She'd become angry when I refused to give her any and reverted to accusing me of being superior. I went a different route and tried to see if she would stay at a women's shelter until she was able to get back on her feet. That was a bad idea, I pretty much added fuel to the fire at that point.

Courtney's behavior was getting noticed by a lot of people, to the point where someone eventually called the Department of Children and Families on her. The day I had to drive her to the courthouse and wait outside while her and the kids went into the court room reminded me of foster care and going through the same motions with Lynn. That was the moment I started to become furious with my sister. We were given a better life, a second chance, and, to me, her children shouldn't have to have court rooms and social workers as a part of their memory. The idea of passing on generational trauma felt wrong to me and at the time I couldn't get over the fact that she could allow that, but the truth is, it's easier said than done; for many it's hard to heal and cope with what happened to them. The trauma didn't start with Courtney and she was passing it on in the way she knew how. After our mom passed I'm sure it added onto the pain she was already carrying. She was being buried in it and I can see how at the time it was hard for her to understand what was going on, the same way I couldn't understand how getting a tattoo wouldn't fix my depression.

After I dropped her off that day what talking (or yelling) we did do went down to pretty much zero. It stayed that way for years; if I wanted to see my niece all communication would be through her husband. Not to be selfish, but in a way it was good timing for me because after that a new set of challenges would come to light.

I was in a light sleep when my phone rang one night. When I picked it up, it took me a few minutes to figure out who was calling me and when he said his name it felt like ice had been poured over my skin. It was Robert. This was our first time talking in five years and he was talking to me in a conversational tone, like we had spoken the day before. He let me know he had been released from prison and wanted to be a part of my life. He had found out about my mom, and said he was sorry. Sadly, since being released from prison he found himself homeless and was living downtown in a lot between Panera Bread and 711. I knew the area all too well. I passed it on my nightly runs through the park after work. The lot was a green empty field that would slowly fill with sleeping bags as the sun set. He asked me to meet him, and I said no. We hadn't spoken in years. I was shocked he had my number and let him know I was not at a point in my life to meet him. The next day at work I started looking up his records and noticed life was hard on him after growing out of the system. Before he called me that night he had been in and out of prison for drugs, armed robbery, and breaking probation. Before seeing his record, I knew he had backflashes from anger but seeing what he was in jail for scared me. I knew not to meet him alone from advice my mom gave me years before, but I couldn't sit back and let him be hungry or cold.

The next day on my way to work I drove by the lot thinking I would see him. It was cleared out by then but just knowing that was where he slept broke my heart. I started to have a panic attack and the next thing I know I'm hyperventilating to my friend Shannon in the work parking lot. We came up with the excuse that I was sick and had to go home. I was living with my friend Rose at the time and after explaining his situation she asked if I wanted help passing out blankets. It hadn't occurred to me, but that was exactly what needed to be done.

From there our other roommates and neighbors joined us in gathering sweaters and jackets galore from people. Shannon was able to hang a sign up at work and in a month we had over ten bags of clothes. We decided to call the charity Box of Warmth; it would provide each homeless person with a hygiene packet and warm clothing in the winter. Because we weren't a licensed non-profit, I ended up talking to the sheriff's office to see what was the best legal way to hand out clothes. Fun fact, I had to go through a church or shelter if I wanted to be safe. Legally, if I gave a homeless person a pair of pants and say they tripped and broke a bone, they could hold me responsible. That wasn't an issue with the church or shelter, and they were ecstatic to receive our trunk-loads of clothes.

The night we handed out clothes at the church was also the night they were running an open food kitchen. Which meant people were getting a warm meal and clothes all in the same place! It was perfect!

As I served food, I realized I couldn't look any of the people in the face. I was terrified to see Robert and have him recognize me, but that thought hadn't occurred to me until I saw someone who looked like him and I froze. I wanted to help but realized I shouldn't have offered to serve the dinner. Luckily someone changed positions with me, and I was able to get away from the crowd. I don't know if he was there that night, but the church was two streets down from the homeless lot he said he was staying in. Box of Warmth was created for him, and we continued to do that for three years. The time went on and the calls from Robert kept coming, but those eventually turned into text messages and Facebook messages. Messages of him getting better and getting work and having a child. He seemed to be growing and that made me happy. He would continue to ask me to meet, and I kept saying no. While I was happy for him that didn't mean I needed to be there to celebrate with him, but he didn't see that.

Avoiding him only lasted for so long though. One night he texted me demanding that I meet him behind a Panda Express after midnight with two warm blankets and if I didn't go, he'd never talk to me again. I didn't reply and instead went straight to my mom's friends, the Mixers. Terry had worked for DCF with my mom and was my main support when dealing with things that were out of my league. He told me not to go which was an obvious thing but said be ready to have Robert blow me up after I didn't show. That is exactly what happened and the next day I went back to Terry's and had over 25 missed calls and voicemails that started off concerned on where I was and ended with Robert threatening to drain every ounce of blood we shared.

He later found out where I worked, started going to my church, and the route I ran, and called me out for telling him I still worked at a grocery store. At my job, Security had his photo on file and when I worked the night shift a security guard watched me walk to my car. I stopped running altogether which was not the best for my mental health especially considering everything I was avoiding. As for church, I took it as a sign not to go back. After losing my mom I was angry with the Lord and felt like he enjoyed watching me suffer. It took baby steps to go back and right when I started that happened, and I didn't try to find another place. I hid my bible in a suitcase and didn't pick it back up again.

Robert continued to call multiple times a day until one day he disappeared again, which lasted for a few years. In the beginning the silence was a relief, but then I began to question where he was and searched his criminal records again. He had eventually ended up going back to jail and his court date was coming up. So, my roommate and I decided to go. I sat in the back of the court room trying to go unnoticed. Then the cop opened the door, and Robert came out in chains with a group of other men. He was exactly like I remembered but at the same time completely different. He was tall and his hair was darker than I recalled. I tried to sink into the bench a little lower, not wanting him to see me. The judge called through names and when his came up words were spoken but I wasn't sure what was said and within thirty minutes Robert and the rest of the boys in chains got up and walked back through the door they came in from. When it was all over, I asked the officer to give Robert a letter explaining I couldn't talk to him anymore, that I was working on building myself and I hoped he could do the same.

Robert never replied and I thought the silence meant he understood.

A blessing that did come from asking Terry for help was he informed me that I had the same scholarship for college as Robert since I was adopted within a certain year.

Say what?

Yup, I had no idea and as it turns out was given free college until I turned 28. My mother never mentioned it and I think it's because she wanted me to work for things and didn't expect me to blow my all of scholarships and Financial Aid. After getting the right paperwork and everything in order I was able to attend full time and went full force.

I'm not going to lie, I loved it. What happened with Courtney and Robert were both situations I should have been talking more about, but I didn't. I was consumed with school and learning, and I was proud of myself for not giving up. Who has time to focus on the negativity and trauma when life is throwing you a party?

Not me.

While that party was happening, I was slowly starting to become un-numbed, if that's a thing.

Which wasn't a good thing.

Well for me.

I was busting through classes at community and trying to transfer to UCF as fast as I could and that helped control part of the sadness due to hyper-focusing on classes, but only to a point. Then December break graced me with her gifts of more time to think, and, along with Christmas around the corner, that unnumbed type of feeling made me want more human connections; so I headed back to Georgia for the first time in years.

I love my Georgia family; growing up I would visit every July for hotdogs and fishing. I would help my cousin with his baseball pitch, and we were left alone to go hunting and exploring in the woods by ourselves. Georgia to me meant adventure and getting dirty and summers meant family gatherings and dancing. I loved it. I loved my family but after losing my mom I stopped visiting them and would tell myself I wasn't a part of their family anymore.

Why?

That BS trauma.

When my cousin Katherine said she'd be in the States visiting and invited me to hang out I jumped at the opportunity for a road trip. I was so excited to be able to visit and see someone. Katherine was the coolest older cousin ever. She was a traveling English teacher who lived in interesting, far-flung places and had the most intriguing stories. To spend as much time with her as I could before she left, I decided to leave after work. The part of Georgia I was heading to was about 7 hours away. I knew I had a drive ahead of me and put on my high school playlist that consisted of Motion City Soundtrack, The Starting Line, Finch, and All Time Low. I grabbed some snacks and headed out. I was making great time and cruising until I noticed red and blue flashing lights behind me. Of course, by this point it was pitch black and the middle of the night in the middle-of-nowhere Georgia. I freaked out, threw on my hazards and slowed down, searching for a well-lit area to pull over that I felt safe at since I didn't trust stopping on the side of the road. Like I said it was late at night and I was in the middle of nowhere. That's how people get murdered. So anyway, I see a road and a hotel and pull off. As it turns out the hotel was closed, and I pulled off into the most isolated area ever. The cop walked up and knocked on my passenger window. Keep in mind Betsy is a 1995 old's-mobile and had roll down windows. I had to take off my seatbelt and reach over to roll down the passenger side.

Man oh man, was he angry! He started raising his voice asking what was wrong with me for not pulling over and when I tried to explain to him it was a well-known safety protocol, he said whoever told me that was retarded, and that he was on the verge of calling in back up before I stopped.

You guys... I was about to be in a slow speed car chase without realizing it!

The officer then noticed my seatbelt off and tried to get me for not wearing a seatbelt too. I made sure to remind him he knocked on my passenger door and saw me take it off. That probably wasn't a good idea because he threatened back up on me again.

Darn my 5" intimidating physique.

In my mind I kept screaming, *Patricia shut up*, but my mouth just kept being stupid. He wrote me a $200 ticket and then gave me a Super Speeder on top of it. I was not going fifteen over and thought that wasn't okay. For those who don't know what that is, it's an additional fee you must pay the state if you are caught going over the speed limit by fifteen. If you pay your ticket but not the Super Speeder you can still lose your license. Luckily, I was able to get that dropped but still had to pay the $200 ticket. One thing I learned from that experience is you don't speed in Georgia.

I ended up getting to my cousin's around 3 a.m. and luckily, they were up playing games. One of her friends had recently appeared on "Jeopardy" and we watched his video and then played card games. Like every moment with my cousin, I learned something new, tried a new food, and left feeling full of love. On the way home, I decided to stop at the outlet malls and grab some breakfast at Cracker Barrel for the road. A road trip tradition in our family. It would start with the outlet malls and end with a warm blueberry muffin.

Pure amazingness.

The drive home was slow and involved a lot of pulling over to look at flowers. I didn't want to return at first. I felt more at home being in Georgia for those few days than I had felt in the last few years of living in Florida, and I missed that feeling. The trip home helped me stop and analyze a lot of things and I realized I was learning a lot about who I was. My rebel-self had encountered the law, ate, and drank with good people, and I realized I could travel with myself and be in good company alone, but I also knew I never wanted to live in Georgia after that. It's just not where I belong. I did miss them and while I missed the feeling of being home, I realized I would be okay and could make my own home in Florida. Visiting family had refreshed my spirit and I felt thankful for being reminded of the love that existed in my life.

Thank you, Kathrine, for that invite. I don't think you realize how much it meant.

After that trip, life sped up. I had been promoted again at work and was considering moving in with my boyfriend Craig. We had decided to start dating again after both realizing that although we had remained friends throughout the years we were still hanging out together more than with the people we dated.

He sat me down and said if we decided to move forward this time around there was no more turning back and the next time we broke up it would be for good. It was a conversation I needed to hear and one that put into perspective our relationship as a whole.

Before we moved forward with dating again he was still a huge part of my life and was always there when I needed help. Craig handled situations the same way my Mom approached them, by understanding my mistakes and helping me to learn from them.

It didn't occur to me that even while we were friends I kept gravitating to him because he made me feel safe. To lose him as a friend would have been horrible and after our conversation about getting back together I knew to start taking our relationship more seriously. That would mean growing in ways I had no idea how to approach.

It was terrifying, and when we decided to move into together I knew I was in for a lot of change, but I also felt comfortable approaching it with someone who made me feel sane, and who saw me through a part of my life when I considered myself broken.

I know, craziness!

But I'm happy I decided to trust him fully and take the leap.

It was a great time but then one day on my way home from work, I found myself sitting outside of our mom's old house. I didn't remember driving there and was just sitting staring when our old neighbor knocked on my car window. I got out, trying to think of something to explain why I was there but ended up just telling her the truth: that was I had no idea why I was there. I started crying as I said this. Terry lived next door to us for almost five years and her and I had become close. She was a college humanities professor and artist. She did incredible oil paintings and loved plants. She once came over and invited me to watch a plant blossom in her garden. I think it was a night blooming cereus, but I'm not sure. Its flowers opened once a year at night and only for a few hours. It looked so fragile, so tentatively alive in that moment. The next morning it was gone. While I was crying in front of her, she just hugged me, and that squeeze felt good. I hadn't been hugged like that in a long time. She said everything was finally seeping in which is why I ended up there, and I think she was right. With everything going well, I was still feeling lost, but this time it was worse because I wasn't numb anymore.

Damn it.

What's interesting about feeling alone is no one can see it, not unless you tell them. Which as you know, I refused to do, because asking for help makes me feel like a burden. Yay trauma! So, I did what I knew best and pushed down the feelings, instead focusing on what I could control, which was being thankful. It wasn't hard, I get happy over slugs, and I am generally a positive person. What I should have realized was that I was a walking time bomb.

One day on my way home from work, I received a text from an unknown number. It was Courtney wanting to talk. I texted back yes, and she called. What came next was not what I was expecting. She informed me she had tested positive for HIV and was sick. I didn't know what to say and asked her what she needed to do next and if she was okay. That was a stupid thing to ask because she obviously wasn't okay. Then she told me that it was my fault that she got it. If I would have helped her before, she wouldn't be in that situation. I became defensive and reminded her of the women's shelters she had refused to consider at the time. She hung up, after telling me to go fuck myself first.

When I got home, I had a panic attack and told Craig what happened. He wasn't a fan of my sister after her performance the night they took our mom away, but always offered advice on how to approach these situations. He said I should investigate and see if there were any scholarships or programs for people who need assistance with HIV, so I started to look. I found a few things and sent them over to Courtney, but she never got back to me on them or reached back out in general.

Thoughts on Good Grief

Looking back now I can tell getting that tattoo done was my way of controlling something about my body and my identity. My skin, with all its scars, was something I already hated so much because of the constant physical reminders of my past pain. I had no idea how to handle my depression and could feel myself spiraling out of control more and more every day; this time, gel pen flowers didn't seem like enough. Thinking about it today, it makes so much sense: I had spent too long in a place where the objectification of my body was a constant. It had started to affect me, and my sense of ownership over my own body. I needed to feel something and to feel in control of myself, not just continue passively suffering. If that meant impulsively getting a tattoo, then so be it.

When the chance came to visit family in Georgia, I took it without question because I not only needed that human interaction but craved it. Of course, I jokingly told about the situation with the cop and being pulled over. Still, at that time, I needed to get to my destination as fast as possible, and that destination was human interaction with family. I almost needed to get there as fast as possible before they changed their minds. Was that trauma related? Of course.

On the way home, I took my time to return to a dull and lonely life; a heavy presence surrounded that location, and the longer I stayed away, the more time I had to postpone that environment.

That meant frolicking around open fields on the side of the road and picking flowers, finding random fungi growing on trees, and bending over for a closer look. I once again surrounded myself with nature to hold on to a feeling I knew would be lost once the arrival back home seeped into my joy of a fulfilled family visit.

Yes, I had Craig, who was there to help me during this time, but we still lived apart. While we were considering merging our lives into one home, they were still very different, and as you know, I had issues communicating feelings, especially those that made me feel bad. At the time, I would get back from my trip and tell him how amazing it was and how beautiful the ride home was, leaving out the thoughts brought on by trauma over the years. That is something I wish I could go back and change. I don't know what the outcome could look like, but from how he treated me over the years, I imagine it would have been gentle and possibly something I could have used.

Especially considering how he helped me during the transition of becoming unnumbed while also giving advice and a different perspective of how to approach Courtney's phone call. A conversation that took me into a deeper mindset than before visiting my family.

I guess what I am trying to say about this chapter is there were a lot of opportunities that presented themselves for me to speak up, and as much as I wish I could go back and take advantage of them, I can't. However, I did; eventually, it just took a bomb going off to set it in motion.

THE WHISPERS/THE UGLY TRUTH

The thought of taking my own life never occurred to me until after losing my mom. There came a moment where I told myself that if all the people who loved me left me or went away and hated me, then it had to do with me, after all I was the common denominator. I was the monster by just existing and my presence brought nothing but pain to the people I loved. I felt that I was poison, so there was a sense of calm knowing I finally had a way out. I took that idea and placed in it in my pocket out of sight, but the day I tried to act on it I realized I couldn't go through with it. There was one thing keeping me from moving forward, and it was my niece. I needed to make sure Sana was safe and had a chance to show the world her greatness. The thought of leaving her paralyzed me from turning on the car. So, I told myself I would stay until I knew she would be okay without me. I figured it would be a few years, most likely after she finished college. From then on, I slowly started to change my reality to fit my end goal. I told myself I didn't want kids when my dream was once to have 4 strong lacrosse boys. I said it was because of the birth process but it was really because I didn't want to make more emotional ties that could poison and hurt anyone else. At this time, I was in a relationship but knew I could end it before an engagement, so no one got hurt, or so I told myself. Obviously, Craig would have been devastated, but in my mind he deserved better and just didn't know it yet. I figured with me out of the picture it would have helped him see it a bit clearer. Clearly, I was the one who needed perspective! Since it would be a few years I figured I might as well finish school.

The scary thing about this stage looking back was how easy it was to hide it from others. I was able to mask my emotions very well, despite the abject pain I was in. That part of me scares me even now. I realize now how dark of a place I was at, and it makes me want to hug my younger self more than ever.

That girl was exhausted and beaten down and used all her energy covering up when she should have just screamed and let it out. That girl was me and at this time all I wanted to do was scream. Do you know the movie *Garden State*? There is a scene where the two main characters sit on the roof of a dusty truck overlooking a giant ravine, and they scream for what seems like ages. And their screams travel through the vast chasm of that landscape, echoing back at them. That was where I wanted to be. I wanted to be somewhere far away from everyone in an empty, alien landscape, where I could scream at the top of my lungs and release everything that was building inside me.

It sucked.

Shortly after that I had another dream about my mom. I had a dream I was hiking up a mountain, heading towards waterfalls in the distance. At one point I had to make it over a river of alligators that were chopping in every direction. In the dream I was struggling to get past them but was determined to do so and remember a pathway of stones leading up to a bridge. That pathway disappeared when I made it past the last gator. The next thing I know I'm sitting at a table at the top of a mountain surrounded by waterfalls creating a mist below. When I looked at the person sitting across from me it was my mom. She glowed. I remember feeling calm. We had a long conversation – I have no idea what about – but I woke up feeling thankful for that dream. It was the first real one that didn't involve the fear of death in many years.

I think my mom knew I was struggling, her soul saw I was a

weirdo who vividly remembers their dreams, and she found a way to talk to me. Maybe she was giving me her blessing to move forward but, whatever the reason, it helped. That fall, I decided to sign up for my first art class since losing her. After she passed, I stopped all forms of creating and threw all my art supplies away.

When I followed the whispers and signed up for an art class, I remember feeling at home. My love for messy palettes, smudged charcoal, and being surrounded by encouraging people sparked something inside. What started as finding a way back to creativity led to creating for others, which nurtured a joy and excitement in me that hadn't been there for years. That scared me! Like all of it! I loved the feeling of creating again and everything it brought me, but I was rusty. I had lost my natural skills, so I had to teach myself how to draw from shapes rather than just do it like I had always done. That was a curveball, but I was determined – plus I didn't want to fail. That is the beauty of being a people pleaser: you are so afraid of letting people down that you figure it out and make it happen.

As someone who did every part of the group project in fear of someone else dropping the ball, I will say that the people pleaser characteristic can sometimes be cool to meet deadlines, even if it was a result of past trauma.

Sorry to therapists everywhere.

Oh wait, you would ask me to look into why I'm apologizing...

Well, this is awkward.

Moving on!

Signing up for that art class lit a fire in my soul, and after that I didn't want to stop. I ended up sitting outside the advising office for two hours, having threatened them with cookies. I cleared my whole schedule to make sure I saw someone and when I did, I was able to add more art classes without adding another semester. But first, I would be required to get intern hours. Not able to work, do an internship and go to school full time meant I would have to take a month off from my actual job.

After receiving hours, I realized I had no idea what I wanted to do after graduation. I thought I wanted to help kids with Cerebral Palsy but soon realized it wasn't good to always leave work crying. Those kids are stronger than anyone I know, and it takes a strong heart to do work with those beautiful souls every day.

So, I returned to helping online students and being a cheerleader. When I arrived back to my desk there was a surprise waiting from a fellow teammate who heard me talking about a watercolor class I wanted to attend but couldn't afford. She told me to keep it on the hush and to give her a painting as a thank you. I found myself at that class way too early and making a fool of myself to the shop ladies but after that I was painting nonstop. Watercolor wasn't my usual medium, and I needed to know more about it! I painted one thing a day for 365 days to learn the skill. I loved the challenge of not knowing what to do and I felt confident I could learn it. That's the superpower of ADHD. If I want to learn something I can and then I'll be bored with it and move on to something else.

So, for 365 days I went into hyper focus mode.

If the joy of creating again wasn't enough, around that time another girl name Jess I worked with said something to me that I won't ever forget. We were scrolling through Instagram, and I kept admiring other artist's work and stationery to which she replied, "You could totally do it!"

How dare she support and encourage me!

I instantly told her I couldn't and gave her every excuse in the book, and she called me out.

Thanks Jess. We need more people like you.

We talked to students day in and out about following their dreams and taking them seriously. I helped students breakdown their schedules to fit in anything and everything in their day. I researched for them for hours to try and make sure they knew where they could find helpful resources; but I wasn't giving myself the same enthusiasm I deserved. That wasn't okay. At one point in my life, I believed I could work for *National Geographic* with no experience because I was confident in my ability and skills to learn. I needed to find that girl again and it was like the universe heard that thought because a few weeks later Jess encouraged me to sign up for a reading group called "Nice Girls Don't Get the Corner Office." That went into reading *The Confidence Code* and next thing I knew I was accepted into a Women's Leadership Group and networking with others. Before I knew what was happening, I was graduating, debating becoming a striving artist, and inviting myself to the women's table at work and in my social life.

How the hell did that happen?

When the hell did that happen?

The week leading up to graduation was mostly me checking over and over to confirm I did it. I kept thinking they made a mistake and wouldn't call my name.

I was thrilled to finally be at the finish line but couldn't breathe until I had walked across the stage. The day I went to pick up my gown and tickets I ended up waiting in line with a few other graduates since the doors weren't open. I had my headphones in but wasn't listening to anything – sometimes I like to have them in as comfort. Anyway, two graduates were talking about their time there and how it took one of them almost five years to graduate, how if it went any longer, he would have dropped out. They then started saying it was embarrassing to take longer than that and people should just give up. By this point I was going on six years for graduation and just smiled to myself. I didn't care that it taken me so long to get there and kept thinking of what my mom used to say about me: "If you want the job done right, ask Patricia. She'll just be picking wildflowers along the way." A quote that used to annoy me because I hated that I did everything slowly, but at that moment it made me smile. I really do pick wildflowers along the way but in my defense those wildflowers were the moments of joy I appreciated along the way of a challenging path. And if anyone thinks you should give up after however many years of working towards something bigger than you, tell them they've got it all wrong. You are doing it at your own pace and that is beautiful! So what if it takes someone ten years to finish school. The people making fun of your timeline have nothing better to do with their lives than put down others and personally I think those people suck balls. You are working on bettering yourself and that's beautiful. Take your time.

After I grabbed my cap and gown, I sent a picture to Jane and went straight to the craft store to get glitter and flowers to decorate it. It would say, "I was told there'd be cake." I had given my tickets to my aunt and uncle Jane and Fred, The Mixers, Sana and her stepdad, my friend and Craig. They were the people who helped push me along and believed in me through the journey. The day before the ceremony, my phone rang.

It was Courtney, it was the first time I had heard from her in two years, and she congratulated me. It was very nice and unexpected, but she said she was getting better and wanted to know why she wasn't invited. I told her I was proud of her for working on getting better and that I didn't have any more tickets, but how the day was for celebrating with the people were on my journey with me. She took it well and understood. She said she was going to try and build my trust back up and be more a part of my life. It was not what I was expecting at all, but I was open to the idea of letting her back into my world.

We continued to text back and forth, mostly little things like what she was getting the kids for Christmas and what she was doing with her hair. After the holidays we didn't talk much, and I went on with my life. She never reached out after that but neither did I.

It happens.

After graduation life slowed down. Most people love that, but let's not forget I thrive in chaos and slowing down wasn't something I could fully understand. Commissions for my art had been growing gorgeously, and I say that in a shocked way. I hated my work and knew I could do better, so every time someone asked for a painting I was dumfounded. In the beginning of my journey, I had made friends with other artists and when they wanted to know if you were someone who showed up ready to learn and grow, you bet your butt I was there! If that meant teaching myself Photoshop and Illustrator in less than a year then so be it!

Yay ADHD!

Those artist friends lead to joining a unique creative community within the artist world in Florida, which meant I had access to resources galore! Before I knew it, I was selling greeting cards, wrapping paper, and art prints and was blessed to be on a podcast to help grow my business. If you don't know it, I highly recommend it – it's called

Brand Therapy. Everything was falling into place, and I kept having moments of courage that helped to push myself further. Those acts of courage lead me to my first licensing deal with the Orlando Science Center.

The two people I had become close with within the stationery world were magnetic, talented women, and to be a part of the journey with them made it feel like the world was ours and we could achieve anything. For the first time in a long time I was confident in what I deserved.

I was networking like crazy and found myself attending local magazine pop ups to make connections. The first one was scary! I discovered the event at work and would have to go straight there after I finished if I wanted to make it. Luckily, I was wearing one of my favorite outfits. It felt rock 'n' roll, but polished: wearing black from head to toe with a pair of killer platform boots, topped off with a slash of red lipstick. After I parked, I realized I had gotten there right when the event started! Yes, I was that person. So not rock 'n' roll. I went to the bar and looked around while the workers set everything up. Luckily it was happy hour, and it was crowded. I saw this girl sitting at a high top table by herself with a drink and I walked over and asked her if she was there for the magazine pop up. The death stare I received from her! It was like I had pushed her grandmother down the stairs. She replied, "Does it look like I'm here for that." My stomach instantly sank, and all my confidence went in a snap of a finger. I walked away, went straight to the bar and asked for a Maker's on the rocks.

I was so nervous that after I paid for my drink, my emergency contact list fell on the floor under the man's chair to the left of me. The same man who, earlier, had tried to charge me to sit next to him – I told him to send me an invoice. I decided it wasn't worth it and by this point the pop up had other people there and were giving away goodie bags. After signing up for the raffle and grabbing my samples I walked around. That was when I saw who I'd like to look like as I grew older. This woman was stunning; she was wearing a floral jacket that looked like something out of Audrey Hepburn's closet. All she needed was white gloves. I couldn't help it and had to tell her how beautiful her coat was, and she invited me to have drinks with her and her crew. By the end of the night, I had learned about her travels, been invited to her garden, and introduced myself to one incredible lady, on top of meeting a lot of local companies.

It was a time of nothing but glitter. That may sound weird but that is what it felt like. Like I was dancing in a room of kaleidoscope lights, underneath the disco ball, with radiant particles of glitter floating in the air around me.

I was building my life to be exactly what I always hoped it would be. I was putting in the hours and work and seeing the change within myself and those around me. For the first time in a long time, I felt like I was becoming a woman my mom would be proud of: someone courageous who knew her worth, but most of all someone who knew how to use her voice. Surrounding myself with confident, driven, and kind people again helped remind me of those things, and learning how to be the best version of myself galvanized me. I wasn't just the girl who applied for *National Geographic* now, I was becoming a woman who not only sat at the table but was also sending out the invites to other women.

And I knew exactly how I got there.

At one point, I had even gained the confidence to attend church again. Crazy, I know!

My first Sunday back in a church, the pastor talked about life not turning out the way we planned it and how the things we had in our life now were a blessing; that we should stop trying to change the past.

It was a great service, and the message he preached in his homily wasn't wrong. Even so, something about it struck a nerve with me. I knew my life was a blessing even with the trauma I had gone through, but personally I didn't care to hear a message about how I should be thankful. I was thankful. I was thankful for my life before my mom died and I was thankful to finally be back in a spot of growth to get that life back. My issue wasn't with being thankful. I was still struggling with the big man upstairs throwing everything and everyone I loved in my face and then taking it away from me. So, when I heard I should be thankful, I was annoyed.

As annoying as his message was to me, attending church that day did hit home in a different way. That was the first time in years I had been physically in a church and you guys there is something about that feeling that is indescribable. It feels like home and like no matter how long you've been gone the doors are wide open. Not all churches have that and when you find one that does, hold on to it. That feeling filled me as I raised my hand and fell back into an activity that once came so naturally to me: the act of surrendering myself to God. But, this time it felt awkward in the beginning and I could only start with one hand. It wasn't until the end that I felt comfortable enough to raise both because I was ready to be home even if I felt like the message was irrelevant. A feeling of being vulnerable to the Lord once again, it just took being in his house for that feeling to come back.

From there it was learning how to be a well-watered woman in faith again, trusting the Lord but this time for real, trying not to cuss as much, and sharing the gift given to me with the world. That was easier said than done but I continued to attend and eventually started making other connections and you guys... I bought a new bible. I had hidden my other one so well that I couldn't remember where it was, and tore my room apart trying to find it.

After my new bible arrived, I found my old one hidden in a suitcase that also held old photos.

I was so excited and went to show Craig. When I opened it up it said, *this Bible belongs to:* Courtney

What the H-E-Double-Hockey-Sticks is this bull and where was my bible?

CONCLUSION PART OF 'THE WHISPERS'

I would never find out where my bible was, but along the way I found my faith. After all those turbulent years, my relationship with God was fractured and it took some time after my return to church to start sorting through the rubble. It wasn't easy, and the more I reckoned with the profundity of my hurt and confusion, the harder it got. This was, of course, completely normal, but at the time I was frustrated with myself. There were plenty of people at church who, despite their own suffering, kept what seemed like unwavering faith. To me they were well-watered women and men who read their bible every day and knew to turn to the Lord when times became hard instead of running away in anger. They were the people who had the perfect relationship with God and could cite you their favorite bible verse without having to search for it. I know now that this was simply part of my journey, and all of that soul searching and prayer helped strengthen my belief and conviction. And that, my friends, is something I am truly thankful for.

Does that mean I am now one of those well-watered women? No, but I am learning every day and, just like approaching my trauma, I have to give myself grace. For me, it's been a constant conversation with the Lord on if I am actually letting him take control of the wheel of my life or whether I'm trying to control the situation again. It's a never-ending battle of trusting him, but that battle seems to get easier every time.

It's a life I know I want and have become more open about with those around me, and what's beautiful about this journey is it's filled with people who help me get there. There is no longer the fear of asking a stupid question on whether or not my thoughts are okay, because I have a great support system reminding me to stay strong.

Those women who surround me have become more than just someone to turn to when needing assurance in my beliefs. They are a community who have witnessed my journey and helped build me up over some of the most challenging years of my life, and those same women cheer me on every day. They encouraged me to follow the whispers and start a business, go to church, and then write a book. When I faced challenges, they were always there to lend an ear and share some advice and when one of those challenges was thinking I was making a mistake after such a long journey of writing, they reminded me to stay strong and keep my eye on the goal, which is to share my story and hopefully help those who find themselves in the same situation.

This was a goal of mine that started as a whisper and then turned into yelling after so many events happened. I think that was the Lord getting tired of sending me signs; eventually He grabbed the megaphone.

But really, if you have something you want to get back into or even try, I say do it and when you fall down don't think of it as failing. You didn't fail, the thing you tried doing failed and now is your chance to improve it. That can be with your faith, starting a business, writing a book, or even making the perfect blueberry pie. One of my favorite quotes is from Ira Glass, where she talks about the gap phase that happens when you're a beginner and how a lot of people don't get past the gap stage because after the first couple of years of trying they realize their stuff isn't that good or up to their standards. Ira then goes to talk about the hard work that one must do to overcome quitting at that stage, namely working more, putting yourself on deadlines to make sure you are working through the volume of work that needs to be done until that gap is completed and your work is as good as your ambitions.

If this quote ever had a face, I'd like to think it was mine, because like my mom said, I really do like to pick the wildflowers along the way, but the point is I was still making strides to the finish line, or, in this case, the next chapter.

Whatever you decide to do remember that it will take time and that you are the greatest project you will ever work on. It's okay to do it with a messy bun, peanut butter on your face, and maybe a cup of coffee that has been reheated four times now.

INTERLUDE: A DASH OF THIS AND A SPLASH OF THAT

Do you bake? If not, let me share some advice: when the instructions say to mix dry ingredients first and then gently combine them with the wet ingredients...

Follow those steps exactly.

The first time I went to bake something that required this, I thought it was silly and mixed it all at once. Of course, the batter didn't come out right.

The reason for those separate steps is because the dry disperses a chemical reaction amongst the ingredients that releases a raising agent.

Obviously.

So, I ended up with a bowl of hot doughy mess, but I learned my lesson and never did it again.

I'm sharing this with you because these next few years felt like God forgot to separate the ingredients, leaving me to deal with the mess.

So, grab a dish towel and let's go, partner.

Chapter 8
THE ONGOING DING

8

There are some noises you hear so much that even when they aren't there... they're there.

Like the continuous noise of a register beeping or an alert for an incoming call at work. Your brain hears it so much that eventually you randomly hear it even when you aren't working. Then, they eventually stop until you hear an odd sound that reminds you of it and are taken back to the days of answering phones in your customer service voice.

Good times.

That was until I encountered a sound that not only haunted my dreams and randomly throughout the day but one that caused me to stop breathing without realizing it.

That sound was a ding: one day it started, and then didn't stop.

Ding.

DING.

DING!!

My first thought when hearing this noise was, *What the actual fuck and who in the world was blowing up my inboxes on social?!*

It was Robert.

Shit.

In the beginning he understood I didn't want a relationship and was working on myself. He would follow up with me and tell me about his successes and wins and I truly was proud of him. It isn't easy to pull yourself out of a bad place, but he was trying and that gave me hope. After I'd tell him to please leave me alone and he'd stop messaging for a few weeks and then would reach out again. In the beginning it was telling me about his wins, his daughter, his girlfriend; then he wanted to know my favorite sports teams. The whole time I'd be ignoring him and occasionally I'd leave the same message in reply, which was: I wasn't ready.

The messages continued and became a part of my daily social life. His presence started to affect my dreams, my emotions, and overall mindset. I had written him a letter and thought he understood but here he was again asking to be a part of my life. Normally I could have continued our ongoing conversations and dealt with it, but I was not given time to figure out how to approach the situation. Not even a few weeks after Robert's message I got a ding from my mom's friend Jane as Craig and I were heading out to go birthday shopping.

She asked me if I had heard from Courtney or saw her being active on Facebook.

Obviously not since we weren't in contact, and Jane knew this.

I checked her Facebook and what do I see?

RIP COURTNEY. *You will be missed.*

It was like it was happening all over again. Like I was reliving my mom's death announcement and the emotions that filled me were nasty. Sorrow and an overwhelming feeling of dread took over but at the same time something told me not to panic.

It didn't feel real, but this time I was in a right mind set and could tell it didn't feel real because something was up.

By this point, Courtney's husband had called me too and I was reaching out non-stop to her phone. I had reached out to a few of her friends on Facebook messenger and tried to search Google for any recent deaths in the area. I couldn't get a hold of anyone and couldn't find anything online.

By this point my stomach was turning inside out and then my phone rang.

It was Courtney.

She was sleeping and started yelling at me for being dramatic and waking her up. She claimed it was a joke but then changed her story and said she was hacked. I was no longer angry with her, but furious. I hung up the phone and demanded we went shopping but was so mad that I threw up. The fact that she also lost a mom and had the nerve to fake her death as a joke pretty much confirmed I didn't want anything to do with her anymore.

This was the first time I had been dealt Robert and Courtney at the same time and yeah, I was not ready for that party.

During this time, I felt safe and was building a life for myself that I wanted but most of all deserved. When they both came into the picture at the same time it was hard to suppress my feelings and I could feel myself becoming unbalanced again.

Craig encouraged me to find a trauma focused therapist. I sent out probably five or six emails to local therapists but never heard back from any of them. Then one night I couldn't sleep because my brain was going a thousand miles an hour, so I decided to paint. It was the ocean, but it showed how I felt better than any words could in that moment. I felt like I was floating out to sea in the dark. The only light I could see was what was around me and into the distance was pure blackness. After finishing that painting, I sent an email to another therapist at 3 in the morning. She replied instantly. She was out of network and because I saw her twice a week in the beginning, I ran through my Eflex card and had to put her on hold after a few months. Right before I left, she told me to keep ignoring Robert's messages, and to not read or respond to them. I told her for sure, I totally wouldn't! It wasn't like it was eating at me at all.

If you're wondering why I didn't block Robert, the simplest answer is because that way I could see what he was doing. I needed to know where he was. He was watching me which to me meant I needed to watch out for him. So, I did what she said and ignored him, but from a distance. That worked for a while but mostly because I was hyper focused on building my art and trying to get out of a job that left me crying three times a week. My determination not only helped me teach myself Photoshop and Illustrator, but I was also figuring out SEO. I feel like the word "drive" doesn't express how hard I was working to make something of myself. It was almost an obsession and every time I figured out something new that obsession grew. Craig was impressed. He said it really showed when I put my mind to something, I go for it. When I told him I wanted to have an actual business and try to get my artwork on products he said he knew I could do it if I had my mind set on it.

Talk about encouragement!

It's a good thing he asked me to marry him on a fun hike through beautiful magnolia trees with our friends one day.

Like that little engagement announcement I just threw in there?

Yup, he popped the question and I know what you are thinking... Didn't you say you'd end it before an engagement, so no one got hurt?

Well, I did say that, and we will address that soon.

At this point though I said yes and had also decided to take the leap and turn my side biz into an actual business by registering it as an LLC. Greg's aunt is a lawyer and luckily she helped me understand how to approach the paperwork for setting up an LLC. His cousin is a licensed artist whose work has been in hotels and more, and they told me all about tradeshows, and how important they are in putting your work out there.

The idea of tradeshows made me sick; I wasn't looking forward to putting my passion project on display, but if that was the way to do it so be it! Not even six months into becoming official, I was featured in the *Stationery Trends Magazine*. It was a moment where I realized just how far my hard work had taken me, which only spurred me on to keep creating.

Starting a business was exciting but it also had many challenges and lessons around every corner. Most of the time, it was a hot mess; it took a lot of late nights researching, driving around town, learning paper types, and lots of tears. You know, the kind of thing one can expect when starting something new. Honestly, I loved that stage. I'm a sucker for figuring things out. However, I didn't consider how hard starting a business would be while also planning a wedding. I would have rather taken my masters than plan a wedding. I had originally wanted to elope, since the idea of a traditional wedding wasn't for me. I fell in love with Japan one day during a research hole in my high school library. When I saw their gardens, I knew I needed to visit. I decided I wanted to get married under the wisteria garden in Japan with my best friend and our parents. Then after we'd go on our honeymoon and explore the trails. After losing my mom that wedding image become a lot lonelier, and so Craig and I decided it would be the place we could renew our vows. Instead, I started planning a traditional wedding; the best part was that I got to make our invites! I had no idea what I was doing and was so excited to learn the process. I knew I wanted dusty rose paper and vellum, and for them to be simple yet exciting. Learning the difference in paper weights, all the shades of black, and how many stamps are Post Office-approved turned out to be a heck of a time! At the same time, my art business was slowly opening the door for custom wedding stationery and so I was still creating content that still helped my business. I had a system down and started to feel like I was made to decorate weddings and run a creative business. At one point, another bride on social media reached out complimenting my organizations skills and asked me to be the coordinator at her wedding. I thought about it and wanted to take it so bad. But, my realistic fiancé Craig reminded me I was planning our own wedding, and trying to build a business, all while working full time. I soon realized that taking her wedding on too might be a bit much. So, I said thank you but no. Even thought it was the right call, I still get excited that she asked.

Instead of flying to Colorado to be the day-of coordinator, I went back to crying over misprinted addresses on envelopes and numerous attempts to correct my printer. It was a lot of fun and looking back it's now hilarious thinking about the number of the breakdowns I had. I had a lot of support from the creative community and other stationers would give me advice on how to approach certain topics like bulk printing and tax prep. There was a lot going on, but it was a good chaos that I felt like I thrived in, and I loved the community that came with it. It felt like I had found a place to plant my roots and was ready to blossom. I loved working towards something bigger. The idea of being my own boss and creating for a living was no longer a dream but a reality that I could taste.

Then,

DING

DING

DING

DING

DING

DING

When I went to check what the notifications were, I froze.

Ten photos of mine had been shared from my account. I clicked on the first one.

Robert had shared my post and pictures on his page, along with a paragraph about a memory he had of us together and how he couldn't wait to meet Craig over dinner. He was no longer just sending me messages but sharing my photos on his Facebook profile. The image that made me sick to my stomach was the one he shared of my little niece and I outside of my new church a month before. That hit different. Everything before this moment was between us two, but now I was furious and terrified that he had shared a post of her. She was still young enough to not have Facebook, so I didn't have to worry about him reaching out to her directly, but I wasn't sure what to do.

Was he watching me again?

Did he know where she went to school?

I needed to make sure she wouldn't talk to him if he found her. My brain went to everything dark that could happen to my niece in that moment – the anxiety and worry for her safety was my only concern. That feeling... that feeling is like someone tied you to a brick before throwing you in the water and no matter how hard you fight, you're going down. Whatever I said to Robert, he wouldn't give me the distance I needed so much.

So once again I told him that I didn't believe it was best for us to rebuild our relationship and if anything changed, I'd reach out. He said he understood and then asked me who my favorite hockey team was. He didn't take me seriously at this point. And honestly, before that photo I don't think I took myself seriously, so why would he.

He kept sending messages asking how I was, and updating me on his life. After sending him another reminder to leave me alone, I continued to ignore them like my therapist suggested. Despite this, silently watching the message number go from 5 to over 20 made it seem like he was all around me. I needed to know what he was saying because it was the only way I felt I had some control. I had nightmares that he would show up at my door or while I was at church or grocery shopping, or that he would hurt the ones I loved to get my attention. Once the nightmares started, I was probably sleeping four to five hours max. Some people can live off that; I wish I could, but I have the energy of a bee and the sleep pattern of a hibernating bear. With the lack of sleep and continuous feeling of fear my emotions were getting harder to control.

To give you an idea of what I was feeling let's say my emotions are the seasons. And inside me every season is happening at the same time and fighting for the spotlight.

Those seasons would eventually be the spark to the suppressed ticking bomb. But not yet. By this time, I was finishing up Women's Leadership and had designed a pin for the graduating class. After presenting the pin to the leadership board, they asked me to give a speech about what it represented.

When they first asked me, my instant reaction was "Sure, no problem!"

GULP.

I was a strong independent woman who knew my worth and knew I could do it!

Stage fright? Nope, not me.

Okay maybe.

Now my only concern was, what do I say?

Luckily, I was able to write from the heart after I found myself face-to-face with an old friend who used words like *pathetic*, *coward*, and *no backbone* – all of them towards me.

After that conversation I walked away from the friendship and wrote my speech the next day. The day I stood on stage I made sure the women knew the pin represented community. To spark conversations and inspire woman to build each other up. That when strong women come together, movements can happen. Who knows where they will be a year from graduation, but as long as they keep working hard, believing in themselves, and surrounding themselves with good, kind-hearted, driven women and individuals, it will make a difference.

I talked about how we were all unique individuals with a similar goal just like a sports team. That the power of a team and community helps not only support each other to step beyond their comfort zone and pursue their passion, but it was also a place to turn when overcoming adversity. When we work hard to support one another, amazing things happen.

I met women in that leadership class that intimidated me at first, but who are now my biggest supporters. Women's Leadership was a team of women who wanted to radiate with self-fulfillment and feel confident enough to make connections with one another. Those women helped me carry myself in a way that demanded respect just like my mom taught me to do, and I had found that those women in that group supported the values & instilled the confidence I needed. I hope everyone can find a group or community like this because it helped me more than I expected. I mean it ended with me literally giving a speech that ended with, "You get a pin, you get a pin!"

What more could I ask for?!

After Women's Leadership ended, the wedding took over pretty much everything and I soon found that the best way to not go crazy was to workout. Working out melted my stress away, which made it easier to approach tasks during the day. At this time, I was doing morning painting stories on Instagram that went over different watercolor techniques and fun ways to use texture. My videos brought viewers into my creative world and favorite activities like running in the rain. I loved making these, but it was getting harder to do if I didn't work out every day; I felt like I couldn't get into the productive zone. I could tell my energy was running low from wedding planning, working full time, and building a business (don't forget those suppressed emotions). I was on cloud nine with all the excitement but needed sleep, and because my brain was always going to dark places with Robert, I barely got enough. If that wasn't fuel to throw on the ember of my suppressed feelings, I don't know what was.

I started to become paranoid about what I was posting and sharing on social media, especially about the wedding. I turned my pages private and stopped talking about the wedding on my platforms as much. The New Year was around the corner and the wedding was coming fast. One of my favorite trends I hopped on the year before was the Word of The Year trend. You give yourself a word that represents what you want your year to look like. For example, my word going into 2020 was *courage*. I wanted to have courage to get more involved in the church, take more leaps in my business, and to be a good wife. 2020 was my year to see where hard work and courage could take me and I was ready to go on a grand adventure! Or so I thought: once 2020 hit things got weird, as you know.

The Lord had other plans for me than I thought when I said courage. I don't think he read the details of my prayers but, hey, he delivered life events that would require fortitude. All those feelings I had been pushing down would resurface very soon, requiring me to draw on something deep in the core of who I am... drum roll please... COURAGE.

Thoughts on the ongoing ding

As much as I would love to say this chapter is long gone and I no longer think about the ding, the truth is I can't. I still hold my breath when I hear a Facebook message come through or see a reminder of messages sitting in my inbox. For this reason, I don't check them as often and wait until there is nothing, I need to worry about going on in my life just in case. I know it will go away in time, but it will be something that will fade like my scars.

As for the fake death of Courtney, that experience brought back a lot of pain from the night we lost our mom and although I'm not angry with her anymore, the truth is a part of our relationship did die to me that day. Going through therapy has helped a lot with forgiveness and I'm thankful for that but the same time I was pushing down the emotions with Robert, Courtneys actions brought on more trauma and this year of my life is one that I had to dive deep into conversation with my therapist.

It was a time of excitement surrounded by darkness and after writing this chapter I can see why I was suffocating. My life was getting to a point that my foundation had been laid and I felt like the storms inside me kept it from becoming solid. It's no wonder I was about to burst. Look at everything that was happening to me, both good and traumatizing.

When your mental health repeatedly gets broken down, there is a moment where it just becomes a part of your daily life. Without knowing it, you're living in a toxic environment thinking everything is beautiful or not as bad as it could be. That is where I was. I was used to the treatment and the feeling of fear that it felt like a regular day of drinking joe on the porch. Going through Women's Leadership was a blessing because after being surrounded by so much love and positive conversation I was able to get to a point of recognizing I didn't deserve that type of treatment. I was focused on helping other women grow and growing myself that it helped not only water the seed I planted but made my roots strong so when I did notice what was going on, yes, I was still crying and in fear but I was able to acknowledge it.

If you find yourself in this situation, it may be hard to recognize, but if you're able to see the position you are in, please know you deserve better, and no one should ever treat you in a way that makes you feel small.

I get that now and wish more than anything I could go back and protect myself during those times and block Robert right away. As for Courtney, I don't know how I would have handled her faking her death til this day so I have to give myself grace for the way it was handled at the time.

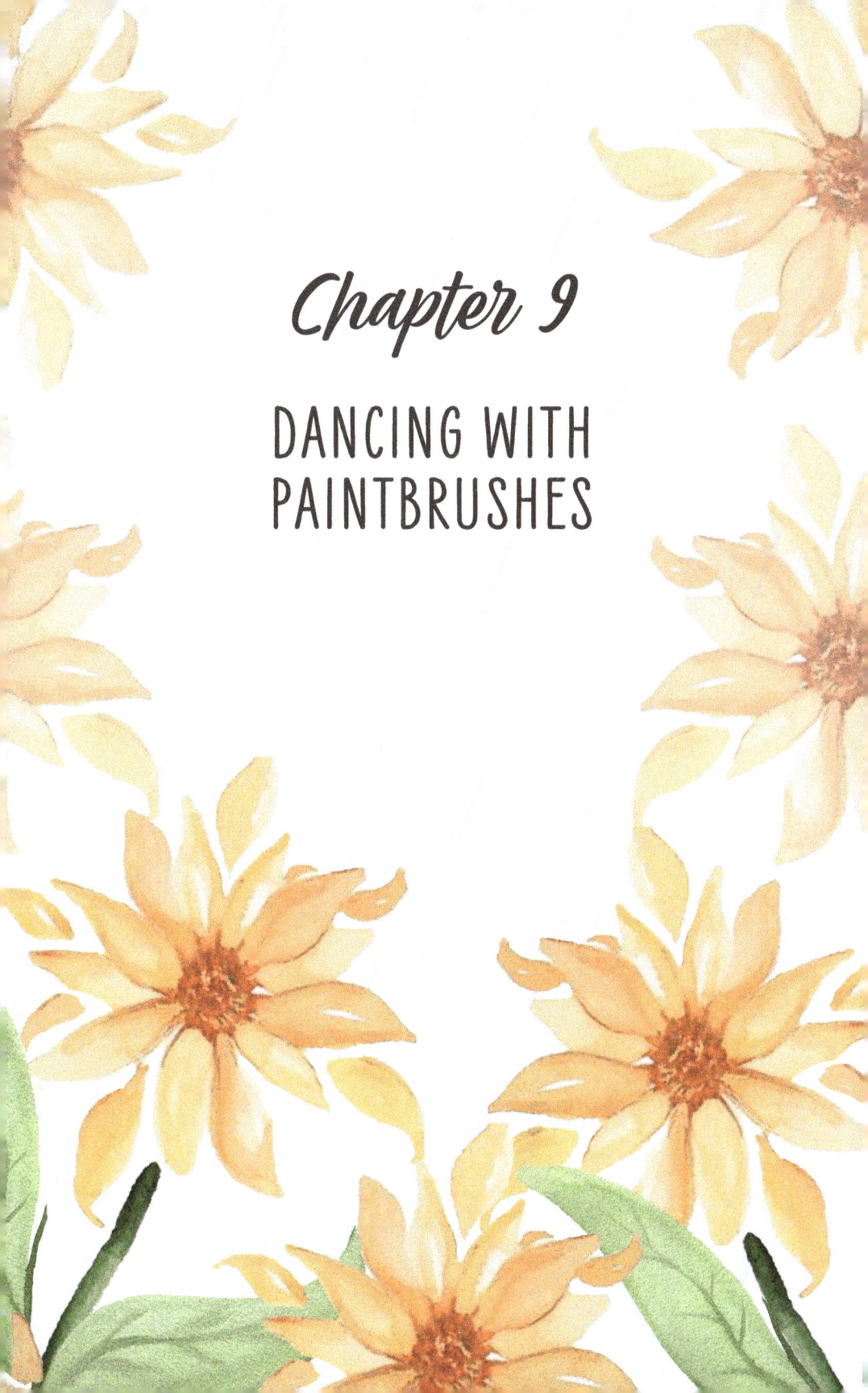

Chapter 9

DANCING WITH PAINTBRUSHES

9

With the wedding around the corner and my emotions slowly bursting out of the seams, working out wasn't cutting it anymore. The day I had to revert to an old trick of love was the last day I spoke with Courtney. She called to congratulate us on the wedding and wanted to know why she wasn't invited. After explaining it was a small family event for our closest friends and family, she told me to go fuck myself again and said she hoped Craig left me at the altar. I wasn't surprised at this point and blocked her number after that.

    I do wish our relationship could have ended in an amicable way, if not continue. She was my sister, and at one point in my life I loved her. To be honest, I was angry with Courtney for so long. She started to remind me of Lynn and that's when I began to resent her. It was while writing this story that I realized that wasn't okay, and that I had a part to play in the deterioration of our relationship, even if I distanced myself in self-preservation. At one point in my life, she was my favorite. She had a future and dreams, and I admired her. I looked up to her for being braver than I could ever be, for knowing what she stood for, and always fighting for the underdog. Her intentions were always to protect, and she had grit. Pushing boundaries were a part of her daily routine and she didn't take no for an answer. She was a tomboy at heart, a fierce ball of Taurus energy that made an entrance one couldn't forget. She went down a dark drug path after our mom died and she couldn't come back. It's heartbreaking to see someone who was filled with so much life get to that point. However, she hurt me repeatedly, and I needed to set those boundaries; I don't know where our paths might take our relationship in the future, but I know that protecting my energy and not just letting anyone have it has given me peace. As of right now I don't want to open that chapter back up. I forgive her, and pray that she gets better because she deserves to be treated with kindness and love and have a beautiful life. But, just like with Robert, it isn't my job to make her happy or to take the blame for the way her life turned out.

After our call ended, I stood there for a bit and just stared at the phone like it was about to say something. It felt like I had just committed a crime and I felt ugly. The last time I had felt that level of ugly was in middle school after the crack-door-shadow-figure memory resurfaced. At least for that experience I knew what the root of it was. The ugly feeling from hanging up on Courtney came from something else that I didn't recognize, but knew I wanted it to go away. Looking back, I believe that feeling came from standing up for myself. Weird, right? I think by that time I was just ready to tell everyone to fuck off, but this time instead of imagining myself doing it, I actually did it and when I realized what I did it made me feel dread.

Before I knew it, my body led me to my paint brushes and acrylics. I grabbed one thin point brush and dipped it in white paint, then let the brush glide over my leg in circular swoops motion as if it was ballroom dancing. The brushed waltzed up my leg and onto my arm; moving its way to my jaw line and then back down my neck to my collarbones. Adding more paint but this time with color, I went over the lines and made flowers and dots followed by hearts and smiley faces. An hour or two later my body was covered in vibrant colors, flowers and love.

Then I hopped in the shower and watched it all wash away.

I started doing this in high school after watching a movie called *What the Bleep Do We Know*!? where at one point in the movie the main character, Amanda, starts to draw on her body after discovering the effects negative thoughts and words have on the body and mind.

That scene was brilliant.

Why didn't I think of that before?! I doodled around my scars all the time, why not continue with the whole body?

I recommend you try it. I love painting my body even when I'm not sad anymore. There is peace in the activity of running brushes over your skin and turning your body into art. During this time, though, I did it because I needed it as a therapy. If you find yourself doing it for similar reasons, remember to be kind to yourself. The situation with Courtney and I would still be discussed in therapy. However, for moments when I needed to remind myself to be kind and gentle, I busted out the brushes and paints.

That helped put my emotions at ease for a little bit. Then, in March, I did something stupid. I opened the messages from Robert and that precipitated the collision of the seasons, it was the spark that set off the bomb, the fuel to the fire, or whatever metaphor you want to use to say I was spinning out of control.

Why did I read the messages you're wondering?

That, my lovely, is how my impulse-control works (or doesn't) in adult version. No longer do I throw clothes over neighbors' fences!

NAH! I now was checking messages I knew I shouldn't at a time when I knew I couldn't take it because... IMPULSE.

That was stupid.

Robert's messages kept repeating over and over and over in my head. I don't know why I kept reading them like the words were going to change, but he was saying everything I feared about myself and confirming it. The little voice in my head, that I did so well to hush over the years, was now on full blast. Things like: *I should have known I wasn't worthy the whole time* and *I look ridiculous aiming for things out of my league*. I was questioning everything about myself and the imposter syndrome was touching every aspect of my life.

With my mind being my biggest enemy and my emotions reaching boiling point I was finding it harder and harder to smile even with so much happiness around me.

Thoughts on Dancing with Paintbrushes

Woah little lady. I'm proud of myself for this chapter. Not for all my action's such as checking the messages that should have been ignored or the way my relationship ended with Courtney but for understanding that I needed self-love instead and curling up and disappearing again. The transition of trying to avoid pain and replacing it with protecting myself. There's an odd feeling that comes to surface, like I was prepared to take both Courtney and Robert on at once for the first time since losing my mom. Like everything I went through with building myself up with Women's Leadership and understanding the strength it took to come out of a hole. As if everything prepped me for the storm, I was getting to sail into without knowing it.

I didn't feel that way at the time. To tell the truth I had a woe is me moment and wanted to know why everything was a challenge when I reached a point of growth.

A mindset that would be discussed in therapy.

THE NOT-SO-UGLY TRUTH

After opening Robert's messages, I found myself at the beach one day. I sat on the beach like I had done countless times before and just listened to the waves. The way they crash into each other and the powerful roar within each break is calming to me. I sat there listening because that was the only thing I could do. A thought came over me as I sat there. Five years ago, I found myself at the same beach deciding to call it quits because of the pain I caused others. That was the first time in almost three years that I remembered my plan I had made to myself at the time. The longer I sat there the more I realized I liked who I was becoming; I was good person who genuinely tried to be kind to others. I'm not perfect but I'm not malicious and the thought of taking my own life for someone else's happiness made me angry. Eliminating myself wouldn't make Robert's life better, nor Courtney's. I will continue to be the villain in their stories no matter what because I'm not who they want me to be. Robert had a horrible life, and it is heartbreaking to see where he is at but that wasn't my fault. I never chose to be adopted. They picked me and showed me what real love is about and what family means. That isn't something I took from Robert, and I shouldn't feel ashamed. I have suffered with survivors' guilt for so many years and I've noticed one thing. He could have been in my exact situation and given the exact family that I had but that doesn't mean his life would have turned out the same way mine did. Yes, I was given love, but so was my sister, and who I am today is because of me and the decisions I've made to be a better person. It isn't my responsibility to make everyone happy. I'm not in charge of their emotions or life. They are.

I realized I would have to stand up for myself if I was serious about not letting Robert back into my life.

That scared me more anything. For one because I knew I had to cut him out of my life and I wasn't sure if I was ready for that, even if he was emotionally abusive in his messages. The thought of him getting better was there for so many years that it was hard to come to the realization that our situation wasn't going to improve.

WRAPPING UP THE UGLY TRUTH

I'm thankful when I look at this time in my life for the people that surrounded me and for God for giving me strength. I don't have much more to say about this other than I'm truly happy that I decided to move forward because if I didn't I would have never seen what beautiful things laid ahead.

Chapter 10

SEASONS GREETINGS

10

A few weeks before April 5th, Craig and I were at a family dinner, calling up venues and pushing the wedding date to October. On the drive home Craig asked me something about the guest list as we were pulling up to the house.

Queue that break-diggity-down please.

In Craig's mind things were hard but we were working through it, and it was okay. In my mind... all the seasons were already in battle, and it was ugly.

Oh, and I should also share that he had no idea I decided to read the messages on top of dealing with the whirlwind wedding.

Maybe I should have left him a post-it...

But I didn't and poor Craig walked straight into a war unprepared!

Poor dude.

I went full Regina George scream. If you know you know.

As I'm screaming Craig was more than halfway out of the car and turns around real fast looking shocked. I threw the car in reverse and flew out of the driveway as he tried to get in front of the vehicle, but I was out of there before he had time.

I needed to escape.

That night I couldn't hold it in anymore. So, I ran, but this time I was behind the wheel. I drove to my favorite park. By the time I arrived, I was no longer screaming and surprisingly not crying, I was just there. The park was dark, and the moon lit up the lake in a way that washed everything in a blueish tint. It was calming and because it was hidden in the back of a nice neighborhood that was surrounded by old oak trees, it was safe and quiet. I sat on the bench tucked away between the trees and cried. I cried because I didn't want to go through it all anymore. I wanted more than ever to run away from everything. I couldn't take it anymore and felt like I was drowning. I prayed because I had no idea what to do and by this time had started feeling closer to the big man upstairs again and hoped he could make it go away.

My mom is totally in heaven saying she told me so.

As the time went by my cries stopped and I sat in silence looking at the moon. I knew I had to go home and that part I wasn't looking forward to since I knew I would have to explain myself. That's the crappy part of living with someone when you don't share all your feelings. They still see them even if you lock yourself in the bathroom or drive away in a panic.

When I finally arrived home, Craig was waiting for me, extremely worried and angry. In my moment of racing out of the neighborhood, I didn't notice I had both of our phones and he had been trying to get a hold of me on the iPad. After apologizing and explaining where

I went, I had to explain the messages. That type of information isn't easy to bring someone into, let alone your future husband. He started to make sure to be careful with opening the front door whenever someone knocked. I could tell it was affecting him, the same way my sister had throughout the years. Things like this didn't happen in his family, which is one of the reasons I fell in love with them all. They're charismatic, eclectic, and wonderfully Greek-Irish. They value family and Christmas cookie traditions. They respect each other even if they talked over one another at family dinners. The way he treats his mom is beautiful. His love language is acts of service and I can't wait for him to treat our future littles with that love. He came from a good family, and always remained sane during these unsound moments for me. I am so thankful for him, but I know both Courtney and Robert took a toll on him. That isn't something I wanted for someone I cared about and loved. With everything going on with the wedding I asked him if he was sure he wanted to get married because I thought he deserved better. I believed he deserved a girl from a family as wonderful as his who grew up with a similar childhood and didn't experience insane situations that were always resurfacing like mine. I continued to give him the out, but he stayed. I think if he did decide to call it, I would have packed up and left for Asheville.

Luckily, work sent us home shortly after my Grand Theft Auto episode; the whole world was being asked to shut down. Now I could cry at my computer and answer calls while laying on my floor in the fetal position. Just kidding – as a floor person, I prefer to lay on the floor with my feet in the air against a wall. I highly recommend it! The benefits alone are amazing!

I felt like I was having better conversations with students and those around me now that I could step away to cry or take a refreshing shower when things got overwhelming. So, after a student yelled at me one day at work, and called me a dream crusher because I wouldn't allow their teacher to extend an extension for the fourth time, I knew how to cope.

Let me crush those mean words with cold showers and 15 minutes walks with my fiancé.

Thoughts on Seasons Greetings

I mean it had to happen eventually! I was a literal walking time bomb and when it did… It was massive. Whoops.

It's a good thing I was in therapy! Can you imagine if I went through all of that and wasn't?! That would have left the world spinning out of orbit and into outer space.

I do laugh at this part of my breakdown. One because I've come so far since then and if you can't laugh at your trauma what can you do?

Sorry was that too dark?

Seriously though, what an experience. It led to so much growth that I never knew was possible and although I do wish I would have gotten to that place without the breakdown that was not the path I chose.

It also helped that everyone was inside, and I didn't have to see people, and that gave me so much time to tackle my trauma and to grow.

It helped me clear my mind and see all of the cards presented to me and because of that I was able to go forward with somewhat of a clear mind.

Chapter 11

GOD SAID 'LET THERE BE COURAGE'

11

The world shutting down was and is still a horrible thing, but it was one of the biggest blessings I could have asked for at that moment. My energy was low and not covering it up with a smile everyday felt refreshing. My mind was planning for an October wedding which I wanted more than ever to be on Halloween. I was extremely optimistic about this date, not realizing how hard it is to book on Halloween even pre-COVID. I was obliviously telling my mother-in-law that the guests would be able to wear costumes, while the poor lady was stressing over me in silence because I was being serious. Just as serious as putting cat nip in my dress so the property cat could walk down the aisle with me.

Have I mentioned how thankful I am for them?

Working from home felt like a weight was lifted off my shoulders and through all of the craziness I somehow landed an interview in my dream department, Marketing.

My interview was over zoom and I can't remember what I wore but I made sure to have my studio in the background looking fierce.

I'm talking color charts on the walls, books on color theory, paint palettes, and a poster for Girl Power to bring it together. The interview went so freaking spectacularly! I could feel myself talking a mile a minute and moving around in my chair while throwing my hands up and expressing my love for connecting with people on social media and being the voice of the university. The notes I had prepared were ignored and things were just falling out of my mouth. At the end of the interview they didn't ask me why I was the best candidate and so I made sure to remind them of how they wouldn't be disappointed if they chose me. Something I did made them like me though because...

I got the job.

I GOT THE FREAKING JOB!!

HOLY CRAP I GOT THE JOB!

WHAT WAS HAPPENING!

They loved me. Turns out they had stalked my social channels for my business for a while and a lot of kind people spoke highly of me for the position. The whole time I was having fun creating and working on growing my business, I had been making a mini portfolio for myself without realizing it. I had the knowledge from great mentors who spoke about brand therapy and knowing your brand, resources galore from the stationery community I was a part of, plus all the random knowledge from my late-night research holes. It all came together in that interview, and as a result my professional life was blossoming. People were noticing the hard work I was putting in and seeing results, and that felt phenomenal. I held on to that win and celebrated like crazy during this time.

Craig and I would walk around the house and say silly things like, "Have you seen a *Marketing* girl around here? Oh yeah, there she is!" It kept me smiling and reminded me of my hard work and that anything was possible.

Craig helped a lot during this time because as happy as I was for my promotion, I was still fighting the voices in my head. Throughout my years of self-development, I realized that I had positioned myself in a place where I truly loved life and who I was becoming. I understood it wasn't me as the common issue, it was a darker evil. The thought of dying wasn't on my mind anymore. But everything I had built for myself was fragile. When Robert's words started affecting my mental health and made me question everything, I feared about myself. I had never felt more like a fraud in my life. The resurfacing thought that I was a waste of space trying to fit into a place I didn't belong kept appearing. I knew I didn't want to disappear and the thought of calling it quits for other people was no longer an option for me. However, I did want to escape. I wanted to run far away and never come back. To be somewhere where there was no pain, and I could breathe. So, Craig encouraged me to reach out to my church, talk to friends, and family. I did, and do you know what they did? They freaking loved me.

They helped remind me of my strength and helped my soul understand that God loves me, my heart, and he sees that I am trying. There was so much love coming from my friends and family, that the negative talk screamed louder in my head more than ever before.

YOU ARE NOT WORTHY

YOU ARE A LIE

EVERYONE HATES YOU

YOU ARE THE PROBLEM

Queue the paintbrushes of love and when that wasn't enough either, throw in some dancing with it.

Robert's messages kept coming and the day I decided it was time for a restraining order was when he called Lynn a coward for running and said Junior was right for never running, not even from the cops.

He had attacked everything about me, and I didn't care to stop him, but when he called the person who I had no feelings for a coward, that's when I switched. While I do believe Lynn is a coward, it wasn't for dropping us off that night. That took courage and I knew that; even though I didn't care for Lynn I appreciated that moment of courage from her. When Robert called her a coward for running away that night it confirmed to me that he wasn't getting better, and I knew it was time for a restraining order.

I called my mom's friend Terry Mixer and he helped me figure out where to go and what paperwork was needed. He informed me I would need Robert's address so I reached out and asked Robert where he lived. He provided it but followed up with, "What are you going to get, a restraining order?" and said that he'd play along.

He didn't take it seriously. I don't think he realized he had pushed me to a point where I was not only exhausted and terrified, but I was pissed. There was anger that had remained dormant in me for years and when he said Junior, the guy who physically tortured children, was in the right, those emotions reacted by mailing him a restraining order by the end of the week.

Thoughts on God Said, Let There Be Courage

I'm thankful for my mom teaching me how to get out of a funk all those years ago through music. That method was one that helped me tremendously and as I've began to heal, I've noticed myself exploring new bands once again. To me that was a moment I knew I was healing and now when I listen to the songs that got me through such hard times I smile because I can see that girl dancing her heart out in the garage trying to understand what's happening, and I know she would be proud of the outcome.

When praying for a year of courage it never occurred to me that part of the process was being honest with myself and the challenges I faced. Getting the chance to get to know myself better was a blessing and one that I will forever be grateful for, because the person I am today is looking back at the trauma filled ready to move forward girl knowing her future is bright and although she was scared she kept one foot in front of the other and never gave up; and that's what led to the outcome of understanding courage and growth.

Chapter 12

THE RESTRAINING ORDER

12

Robert wasn't happy to receive the court papers but, in his defense, I don't think anyone would be.

He continued to message me about how I was making a mistake and committing a crime. How I was as horrible as Lynn and Jr for abandoning the only blood family I had left and the only person who truly loved me. That the decision I was making to cut him out of my life would catch up to me and I'd regret it when God judges me. I thought he could be right, about everything. I felt as though I was as horrible as Jr and Lynn for not wanting Robert in my life and that felt like a knife going straight through the heart. I never wanted him to feel that way, especially because of me. The feeling of abandonment that was created from being dropped off on a stranger's doorstep was a feeling and emotion that took a lot of energy and mind power to get rid of and to think I caused that to someone was heartbreaking. The thought of me going forward with the restraining order began to waver, and I started to internalize the thought that I was committing a crime. What if I got up there and the judge thought I was overreacting or being an emotional girl? Robert was apparently an expert in court and me, I was an expert in crime shows and murder podcasts. I ended up calling my cousin who's a lawyer and explained the whole situation. Keep in mind no one other than Craig knew what was going on because I didn't want to burden anyone, so explaining the whole situation to her was fun. I asked her to keep it a secret and she did. When I was able to open up to other family members about it and explained I was sorry for not telling them, they replied with, "We are here for you and even if we can't be there in person, we can include you in our prayers." They really do love me, and I'm happy that I can tell that now, but kind of wish I knew that after losing my mom but hey, I figured it out along the way and remain very thankful for them.

After I got off the phone with my cousin, I took her advice and started documenting and making notes from Robert's messages. I started gathering any evidence I could, which meant printing out pages of all the photos of mine he shared on his page, and the messages he had sent over the last few months. Once the printing was done I had over twenty pages. From there I started rereading his messages and highlighting and making notes of things I could use to prove my case. The one part I didn't have evidence on was when he threatened to drain every ounce of blood we shared. That was in a voicemail that was long gone. I did, however, have a Terry who helped me through the whole situation and worked with foster children and families who said he'd be more than happy to speak up if he had to.

Documenting took a toll on me. It was nothing like the TV shows. The whole restraining order situation hit me hard, and I was breaking down over the simplest things like not emptying the dish washer. My inner thoughts were chaotic and by the time I started training for my new position I was walking three miles every morning, dancing in my garage at night for hours, and going on walks in the rain with my Craig. The morning walks helped me process everything easier. We lived near ranches and wooded areas, so we were surrounded by nature. Not just any nature, trails that took you into woods that you could get lost in for hours without having to worry about running into another person. Farms that were taken care of by old couples who rode lawn mowers together and made the walks all more beautiful and then parts of the neighborhood that you could run into a bobcat. It was nature and everything I loved minus the beach and it was beautiful and surrounded by kind people. The morning walks included bringing carrots and trying to become friends with a horse who lived on the corner, making friends with a dog through a fence, and learning the early routine of the tortoise that lived in the garden down the road. I declared myself the president of the tortoise watch in the neighborhood.

It's kind of a big deal.

I'd always return home dirty from walking through fields and exploring the creeks, feeling refreshed to take on the day. But I couldn't bring myself to continue to build my brand on social media while processing everything, training for a new position, and still planning a wedding. My family and I decided it was best to step away from my business and social media for a few months and until the restraining order went through.

During those few months I was a wreck. I cried every day and barely slept or ate. My dreams were just nightmares of Robert being upset with me and hurting me. When I was awake, the recurring question of whether I was following the right path or not was ever-present. Looking back at it now, I'm not sure how I handled it exactly, but one way was doing the exact opposite of what I did when I lost my mom. Instead of turning away like I had done then, I asked for help.

And do you know what?

It didn't kill me!

What a win!

As the court date approached my walks became longer, and I danced more. I needed something faster than what I was listening to and put on one of my favorites – Little Richard, "Good Golly Miss Molly." I probably played that song ten times in a row minimum. I would create games with myself that I had to keep moving through the whole song, because someone had challenged me to a dance-off and to win I couldn't stop for a moment. I did this even when I was coping, but challenging myself to win was new. I was rooting for myself. I wanted to continue to be the cheerleader, the creative ball of joy and determined person who believed in magic like I was before. I liked that person and with the help of Craig, my family, friends, and church, I had an army fighting with me to keep her and I felt ready. Terrified but ready.

The day before the court date I decided I needed to go shopping and bought a whole new outfit. A new blazer, pants and top. I didn't want to wear anything I liked in my closet and told myself if he won, I'd burn the outfit. If I won, I'd still donate it because I didn't want to look it. I went with a simple black blazer and pants with a white silk blouse underneath. I would have loved to dress like Elle Woods but figured it was best to keep it simple, and darling, you can't go wrong with a classic black and white color combo! That night I stood at our kitchen bar with a glass of whiskey, and I read through the messages and bookmarks to make sure I was ready for the next day. I had spoken with my cousin to get an idea of what to expect when I got there, since I'm pretty sure that it wasn't going to be like the TV shows. She helped me breathe and gather my thoughts.

JULY 2, COURT DATE

It was a hot July day, but luckily not peak-season hot. Like I had started my day for the last few months, I went on a morning walk. I had to be at the courthouse by 9 a.m.; luckily, I wasn't sleeping so was up at six and still had time to get one in before everything started. I still hadn't built enough trust with my horse friend on the walk to steal him and run away, and I think his owners were catching on to me. I can't help it, my carrots are fantastic, and we both have a calling to run wild.

After returning home feeling ready and refreshed I started getting dressed. Normally I listen to upbeat songs in the morning as I get ready; it's my way of dancing into the day. Not this morning. Playing on the TV so quietly you could barely hear were ocean sounds. One of my favorite things to do on the weekends is wake the house up: I put on ocean views and slowly fill the whole house with the sound of birdsong and the waves crashing. I decided this was the type of energy I needed this morning. Craig made me some iced chai tea and toast as I sat on the floor in a sports bra and shorts curling my hair. The whole time I was curling my hair and putting on my makeup I was reminding myself I could do it and was strong. Then as I put on the blazer and platform boots, I saw that I was strong. I saw me, the woman who believed in herself and knew her worth. I hadn't dressed up like that in a while and while my mental state was fragile, the person who looked back still appeared strong on the outside. By this time in my life, I really had been faking it till I made it in a lot of situations and, looking in the mirror I realized I had ended up making it, which is cool!

The courthouse was about twenty minutes from where I lived and when I arrived, I met my mom's friend Terry. He greeted me with a big smile and played around, telling me to smile and everything would be fine. I guess I didn't look confident after all but now I had Terry so that was okay. Entering the courthouse was a process but we were getting through it, and everyone understood there was a virus killing people, so no one rushed. We were required to take temperature checks and fill out forms before entering the building and going through security. By the time I had got to the inside of the building I was a sweaty mess under that blazer.

Luckily courthouses are always cold, and I dried fast. Nasty I know but that's Florida living at its best for you.

There were a few other people inside the courtroom waiting, and it was just like my cousin said. I would most likely be with a group of people who were all requesting restraining orders and they'd call us up one by one. That is exactly what happened. The whole time I looked around waiting to see Robert. I know he said he wouldn't come but I didn't believe him. As I was waiting for my name to be called, I gripped my blue binder like my life depended on it. Terry noticed and told me to relax and gave me some pointers on how to speak. When I let go of the binder you could see sweat drops from how bad my hands were sweating. Around the same time a good friend from work came and had snuck in the back. I wanted to hug her so bad for being there. She was a part of my Women's Leadership group and related to a lot of my journey. She asked if she could come to provide strength since I wasn't letting Craig. I was afraid that if Robert did show up he could hurt him, and I didn't want to risk it. When she found out she insisted and when she showed, I was so thankful for her.

Then it was my turn. Robert still wasn't there and when the judge asked what the restraining order was for, I said stalking. He looked up and said, "Ma'am this here says it is for domestic violence." I politely confirmed and said I didn't know why it was under that because I had stated stalking, and explained that Robert was my birth brother, and

I was adopted from foster care at ten years old, and that he believed I was brainwashed, and his actions and behaviors are causing me to relive trauma.

It was approved, although if he had been there maybe it would be a different story. But, still, it was approved! I didn't realize it though, and just stood there, not knowing what to do next. The judge said I was good to go, and I started to leave the courtroom, when the cop and judge were like ma'am you need to wait for your paperwork. After throwing the courtroom into a frenzy for not knowing the legal systems exit process, I found my seat and cried again.

After getting in touch with my emotions I've realized at this point I'm just a crier.

Walking out of the courthouse felt like dream. I was ecstatic and couldn't believe it was approved. I didn't look silly or like I was overreacting, and that was huge. Terry hugged me, and said he'd see me soon, and that he was proud of me and then left. After that I stood in the parking lot with my friend for an hour talking about where we were at in life, how we both wanted to build stronger foundations for the future, and sadly about recently losing an incredible soul who was a part of Women's Leadership. She gave me a white crystal and told me to keep it close and then we hugged, and I drove home. The white crystal is considered a master healer and helps amplify energy by absorbing, storing, releasing, and regulating it.

On my way home I stopped at Five Guys and ordered a bacon burger with jalapenos and large fries. When I got home and shared the incredible news with Craig, I ate like I hadn't eaten in months, and then I slept for the first time in the same amount of time.

Thoughts on the restraining order

For anyone going through a restraining order I am truly sorry. That whole process was intense and drains the soul. Something that you don't need while already struggling. You're required to have relevant proof while also gathering information from the person you don't feel safe around to prove to a judge, you're not crazy and need protection and you know what, it sucks. I understand why it's needed and don't mind but that doesn't make it suck less.

However, the moment you learn that it went through is one of the most incredible feelings. The day I went into the courthouse I had no idea what the outcome was going to be and apart of me did think I would end up going to jail. Why? Overreaching, not being a good sister, and wasting the judges time. All things that are ridiculous thinking about now but were real fears that went through my head. When I discovered it was approved I could feel my body relax for the first time in years and after eating that Five Guys Burger my stomach thanked me for feeding it for the first time in a long time and rewarded me with a nap.

When I tell you I slept for the first time in a long time I mean it. The week after the court date I slept about 12 hours a day and felt myself getting back to what I considered normal after. A few weeks after I was slowly trying to get back to my life but it was hard and I found myself sitting in front of my website and business not knowing how to start back up. My mind was ready to take on the world again but a part of me was blocking that from happening. Looking back at it, I know deep down it was time to start my healing journey and the reason I was blocked from starting my business again was because more work needed to get done.

Chapter 13
ONE YEAR LATER

13

Bring on the creating! I somehow pushed myself to get back into working on building my business again and I was back into a routine of working my butt off and loving it. So much so that I kept remembering the restraining order needed to be renewed but every time ended up telling myself I had more time. One beautiful summer day, during my workout, I was deep in my thoughts: planning a custom order, feeling excited to be accepted into wholesale and realizing I needed to work on my SKUs. Then mid-workout I remembered what day it was and ran to the safe in a panic. I grabbed the paperwork and realized I had missed the renewal date on the restraining order and that if I wanted another one, I would have to go through the entire process again. I texted my manager saying I couldn't go into work and the world was literally on fire. Craig drove me to the courthouse. I remember being angry at myself for not prioritizing it, but I think I did it as self-sabotage and acknowledging that part annoyed me even more.

    I needed that trauma behavior to get itself together!!

When we arrived at the courthouse, I was turned away at security for having plyers in my purse (chaos, I'm literally walking chaos). I was working on my keychains the night before and stuck them in my purse for some reason. Luckily my husband returned them to the car and the security guard cracked a joke. As Craig returned the plyers, I found the restraining order room. When I approached the desk and rang the bell, I asked the lady if there was another way of renewing a restraining order or if I had to do the paperwork again. She said I had to do the paperwork again which I knew but wanted to confirm. While filling out the documents I noticed my form said "Domestic Violence" and asked them if there was one for stalking. A new lady behind the counter said there was but my situation fell under the domestic violence category since it was family related. I asked her if there was somewhere I should put that it was a stalking case and explained what happened last year during the court date. She then so kindly said if I wanted the stalker form then I can fill that form out, but it was my decision.

As someone who has worked with a business and understands certain documents are needed for certain categories I found her answer to be rude. We were talking about a restraining order not something trivial like a change of address form. By this time, I was almost an hour into filling out documents since I was so nervous and couldn't remember small things like my address. My patience was nonexistent and when she wouldn't give me a clear answer I not so subtly expressed my displeasure and reminded her she was the expert not me.

She recommended the Domestic Violence form.

After another hour of filling out paperwork I walked up to the desk and rang the bell. I gave her the forms, of course having missed a few places and so had to sign here and there. I had to confirm all the information was correct and lift my right hand. She informed me that the paperwork would be processed and I'd be hearing from them soon. About to leave, I asked her if she needed my old paperwork for the file. She said no but offered to take it. When I handed it to her, I asked her which date was correct since there were two on there so I can know for the future. She then pulled up my file and did a few checks on my paperwork. After she looked them over and checked her computer a few times, she told me, "Ma'am, your case is indefinite unless he tries to revoke it in some way."

Excuse me, WHAT?

My first thought was *are you serious right now*. Why the heck did I sit in this cold and horribly lit Government office with horrible service for two freaking hours when they could have just looked at my file when I arrived!

In the end it didn't matter, because I felt like I could breathe again. Last year was one of the hardest years I've faced, but I put my full trust in the Lord for the outcome, and he delivered.

As we exited the courthouse, it was pouring. It was a beautiful Florida thunderstorm, and I walked right into it happily, heading towards the car. Craig followed and halfway to the parking lot he did a little jog to a nearby bush. He had stashed the plyers in the bushes after the security incident since we were parked far away. In the middle of a downpour we started laughing and I felt a sense of peace.

The rain was rejuvenating, and I felt like it was meant for me. It almost felt like I'd come full circle from that night in the rain as a child. I was safe and I felt like the trauma was officially over; this time the rain wasn't calming a child who had no control over chaos, it was thundering down in wild celebration for a woman who was able to look out for herself.

Thoughts on a year later

There's this quote by Anne Lamott that I think of when looking at my life during this time and that quote is, "I do not understand the mystery of grace- only that it meets us where we are and does not leave us where it found us."

And my goodness is that true. Grace presented itself on a courageous journey and has followed me till this day and for that I am thankful. Seeing how far I've come brings a feeling of overwhelming love and I know it's because I allowed myself grace along the way.

Since the restraining order Robert has reached out to me once under a fake name to remind me God will punish me and that Robert will be the only person who loves me, you know, the normal. I looked at his message and took a screen shot and started a folder but felt nothing after. Not a feeling of numbness but a feeling of knowing he is wrong and God loves me more for my heart but that I also have a community that loves me too . Plus I know I love myself and that no matter what he says he can't hurt me with his words.

Chapter 14

RELATIONSHIPS, FLOWERS, AND THERAPY...OH MY

14

During the healing process of 2021, I started remembering that little girl who was left on the front porch, exhausted and soaked, a memory that's still so fresh in my mind. Writing this book put me in an emotional state of *holy crap, that one night literally changed everything for my life,* and to think it could have gone differently is overwhelming. So overwhelming, that it almost paralyzed my writing. Then I realized that little girl deserves love, and she's me. For most of my life and till this day the idea of unconditional love hasn't made sense when it relates to me. I love my niece more than words can describe and the unconditional love I have for her is obvious without needing to analyze it, but my mind doesn't comprehend how to receive that back. It's something my therapist says will just click one day. It hasn't clicked yet but what has clicked is the love I have for myself. I had been working on my personal growth and started to understand my worth; during that time, I fell in love with who I was becoming. During the restraining order I was reminded to love myself even without accomplishing all the goals I had set for myself and instead was forced to look at who I was as a person. I had to step back and see that girl also deserved compassion and love too. I mean, she was the one working on making a better future for myself, so she couldn't be too bad, right? Well, that chick had some grief. A grief that hid for many years because of the fear of what it meant to acknowledge it. There was a fear of pity from others or sympathy that came with the grief. I didn't want to use it as an excuse. I didn't want people to look at what I went through and think *how disturbing; she's broken, poor thing.* It was shame for being abused. Like what? Is that even a thing?

Apparently it is, because that's how it felt.

To me, the world saw me as less because of the abuse that was out of my control. As if I had asked for an older man to treat my body as he pleased or deserved to watch Robert being brutally beaten in front of me.

Talking about it meant acknowledging those events out loud, and that brought a feeling of deep shame. So, I rejected my story for many years and instead only focused on the good parts of my life. The joy of being adopted even though I felt like I didn't deserve it. I knew I was in a better place and had an incredible mother figure there to guide me. I hid my shame and imposter syndrome by sharing the joy of adoption and using it as my superpower. To me adoption was a blessing and it made me stronger, so I held on to that.

Until the moment someone wanted to know about the abuse, then I'd just brush it off and change the topic to something less dark. What happened to me was no longer relevant so why would I care to focus on it when the feeling it brought was shame?

Looking back, I can see why it's important to talk about it and the truth is, it's going to come up no matter how hard it's pushed down. The longer it sits and is rejected the more it grows until one day it screams for attention.

The events that unfolded with Robert brought that shame to light but this time I couldn't push what was happening away. I had to face it. After understanding that to accept shame and grief was to befriend it, I started realizing that although I endured a lot it didn't change who I was now and if my past makes people uncomfortable that's not my problem. My concern is with myself and letting the hurt have its moment.

After its moment is acknowledged and understood I can move on, right?

It's not that simple, or at least for me. In therapy I was asked to close my eyes and picture a white room with nothing in it. From there I was told to picture myself holding a ball. My ball was a green glass ball that fit perfectly into my palms. I loved it and I thought it was beautiful. From there I was asked to picture a door and open it up to a closet. That door was wooden, and the handles were old. My closet was black and small but at the same time peaceful. I was informed to grab a box from the shelf and place the ball in it. My box was a shoebox and after placing the ball into it and placing it back on the shelf I realized I missed holding it.

From there I was asked to turn around and focus on another door in the room and to describe it. That door was yellow, not my favorite, but this door was an inviting yellow with a glass door handle. When I opened the yellow door, I saw the ocean, and I felt peace.

As it turns out, the ball was my trauma and I was allowing myself to let it go by placing it in the shoebox and back into the old closet. The feeling of missing the ball was a shock to me and I could tell my therapist thought so too, because she wrote things down and said that we'd need to work on that and dive deeper into that feeling.

I am still working this out with my therapist, but I think that the reason I missed the ball was because I was finally able to hold my grief after ignoring it for so long, and once I acknowledged it I began to love it so hard that I thought it was beautiful. Once I was asked to put it in the closet and focus on the door that brought peace, I missed it because to me I had finally just begun holding it. I wasn't sure how to let it go now that I was given the chance to hold it and moving forward to the peaceful door brought a sad feeling. A feeling like I wasn't ready to say goodbye or just wanted to hold it one more time because I was finally understanding what that trauma consisted of and if I went through the new door, would I get that chance to continue to understand it or would I leave it in the past?

To me that meant ignoring it again and I didn't want to do that. That scared me because I saw what it led to and didn't want to go through that again.

The feelings that came from ignoring my trauma for so long made me feel like I was drowning in a pitch-black open ocean. The messages Robert wrote confirmed my fear of being a fraud, and nothing more than an abused foster child whose birth mom didn't even want her. It was like he knew where to stab and hurt me the most. Those thoughts were always there but were silenced from years of positive affirmations from my mom, so for many years stayed dormant. When my mental health started screaming for attention and the messages Robert sent kept replaying in my mind the thoughts of being a fraud burst to the front. Everything in my life became a question and I was started to wonder why I even tried to be better, whether it made me look foolish. My thoughts kept telling me to stop trying and to give up already because everyone was laughing at me and hated me. That the world didn't have a place for someone like me and no matter how hard I tried I would end up a failure. Those thoughts screamed nonstop in my head for months and it involved more rewiring of my thoughts than I had done before, or at least it felt like it. Maybe it was because they were all there at once instead of sprinkles throughout my life. As the thoughts became louder and the grief made itself comfortable, after many years of kicking it out of my mind, I broke down hourly. Dancing for hours morning and night helped me tell those thoughts to shut up and that Robert was wrong. The truth is Robert didn't know me. He hadn't for years and what he saw on social he took and put into his own narrative. The messages he wrote reflected how he felt about himself and while I also had those thoughts, deep down I knew they weren't true. His feelings are valid although the thoughts were wrong. He deserved to be angry because of what he went through, but I didn't deserve to be the one he projected his feelings on. Every time I would feel ashamed or like I didn't belong I had to tell myself that I deserved to be here as much as anyone else and what I have in my life was because of the hard work I put into the world. I had to remind myself that no matter what I deserved a spot and that I was still blossoming into who I was meant to be, and this was just another part of the journey.

And you know what, it was hard. Out of everything I've been through, reminding myself of my worth during a time when I felt the world around me was casting me out was my biggest challenge.

It's funny isn't it?

Trying to love myself and prove my worth to those voices in my head during a time that it was needed most. It felt like more of a challenge than losing my mom, watching my sister lose the battle to drugs, and saying goodbye to Robert.

Here's an example of what my intrusive thoughts were like pretty much nonstop in the beginning. To set the scene let's say I'm brushing my hair after a shower.

Hey there friend! You should mask after this and braid your hair for waves in the morning!!

Sup Loser, remember that time that you picked a roach out of your hair while sleeping on the floor in Lynn and Jr's room? That's disgusting and if people found out they'd hate you.

OH MY GOSH SHUT UP. HOW IS THAT MY FAULT.

Enters emotions:

Excuse me, I need attention.

Oh, hey sadness what's up?

We need to cry.

But I'm literally getting ready for sleep.

No we need to cry and then remember all the details of the room being lit by the moonlight and you itching your head and grabbing a roach and Robert smacking it away.

He's right you know. You are pathetic.

Hey there buddy, you should probably go dance for a few hours and tell yourself nice things.

Queue headache and tears while heading to the garage.

As I continued to nurture the negative thoughts and sad feelings the thoughts eventually got to a point where the running script looked like this after a shower and brushing my hair.

Holy cow my hair is getting so long. Could you imagine how heavy Rapunzel's hair must have been after she went swimming?

I should reschedule an appointment with my chiropractor. My neck hurts.

I can't wait to chop all this hair off when I reach my goal. I should donate it.

Maybe I should I dye it again too.

Sup Loser, no matter how much you change your hair everyone knows you're pathetic.

WOWWW, okay, wtf.

You're just a sad witch who needs love. Come here you noodle. Let me love you.

🌸

The change in that mindset took a year and half to get to but only after allowing myself to feel and scream and yell and cry. At one point I was so angry I beat the living shit out a pile of laundry my husband set up for me in the garage with a hockey stick. What started with me beating the crap out of it led to me crying over it. I cried over having to be strong during a time I should have been allowed to be weak. The anger was from Courtney not being there for me and my feeling hopeless to help her. I was mad at her for not pushing down her feelings like I was able to do, but I also realized what I was also doing to cope wasn't okay. The way we approached our grief was learned from a young age.

The tears were for Robert, a young boy who protected me and wanted nothing but love, having to feel rejection again but this time from me. Those were emotions that needed to be let out and I welcomed them to show themselves. Every day was baby steps and giving myself grace. The year 2020 was a year of being courageous and 2021 was a year of healing from the mess of being courageous. It wasn't easy, if anything it was a hot mess, but I can see why it was worth it now. It's like putting up a judgement free zone in your mind and allowing yourself to have those bad days and not feel guilty or ashamed. When the thoughts that I'm weak for asking for help, that I'm not worthy of love, and a fraud come to mind now I can look at them from my judgement free zone and acknowledge them but move past them with ease. I must treat those thoughts with indifference because that's all they are now. They don't deserve my energy. When this light bulb hit it was like the day I learned about indifference with Lynn. To approach those negative thoughts with a different outlook on love for myself, it turns them into liquid. However, I had to give those negative thoughts an image to defeat them in mind. The same way I imagined Jr on the sun. But what type of image could I give these thoughts that sucked the life out me? If you thought of the Sanderson Sisters from *Hocus Pocus*, you'd be correct.

I know it sounds weird but hear me out. When the negative thoughts start creeping in, I picture myself defeating the Sanderson Sisters with the burning rain of death, aka Love. Sometimes I take them down by giving them daylight savings time. By personifying my thoughts in this way, it makes it easier to approach and defeat them. Sometimes it turns into me laughing because of how silly it is, but hey it works! And what's even sillier are those negative thoughts.

Things were changing in my mind and while the seasons were at war, I was learning to flow with them. The energy that it took drained me, and my days involved a lot of self-care and gentleness. Amongst the seasonal storms happening inside me was the thought that I had to make it because I refused to go backwards. The amount of work put in throughout the years was hard, but I did it and to give all those late hours and achievements away didn't make sense, especially now that I didn't want to end my life, even when I wasn't immediately "needed" or depended on. Sana grew to be an emotionally intelligent high school student living in a different state, a thriving young adult. If I had not worked so hard to understand my trauma and the emotions that came with it, I might have been in a very dark place, feeling purposeless without her dependency as a child. However, after seeing her life blossoming, I felt lighter, and I knew I was okay. She may not rely on me in the same way, but I am always here to make her feel loved more than every speck of sand on this earth and every galaxy in space – and everyone needs that.

Do I wish I would have approached my trauma sooner?

Oh, for sure! But I didn't. I also didn't stop listening to my mom or reading the books she gave me and when it was time to finally approach the trauma, I felt like I had a guide. Coming out on the other end of all the trauma feels different. I am still me, but I am not. I'm stronger than I have ever been and in love with who I am. I love my body and the strength it gives me to still act like a kid, I love my mind for being the most incredible weapon I have, and I love my soul for staying kind and humble like my mom taught me.

Most of all I'm proud of myself for being able to step to the side and let the little girl that is still scared and hiding under that bed know that she is safe and that I will be there for her every day until she is comfortable to come out and see everything that was built because of her.

So, what do I want with my life now that I am somewhat okay with resting and not filling my time up to avoid trauma?

I try to live a beautiful life and one that I know I deserve. Yes, there is sadness once in a while, because life can be sad, but it's also filled with magic, love, trust, and baby steps towards building a life that can be enjoyed by my children.

To me that is setting boundaries with people and allowing myself to be surrounded with those who treat me with respect and love. I no longer talk with Courtney, but she is still a part of my niece's life and I respect that relationship with them because I love my niece. It means knowing that I don't have to let her in just because others do and that doesn't make me wrong. It helps me move forward and keep the life that I've built growing in an upward direction.

I can feel like I am getting to a point of being comfortable with sharing my life again on social and with others around me. Not fully though, and that will take time, but just because I'm not on social doesn't mean I'm not living. At first, I thought this was still giving him power over me but I have since realized it wasn't just that. When I disappeared at first it was for my safety but later it was because stepping away from social media was the only way to work on myself. Self-isolating is a trauma response that was learned early on and one that has gotten better when it comes to those close to me, but just not with social media, and that's okay. Not everything needs to be documented.

My business has turned into this book and has fallen behind on the trends but, honestly, I don't care. This book was more important because I know it will help someone and even if it is just one person, that one person needed it and so that is where the focus has gone.

My days are filled with writing, caring for my garden, rock-climbing, and yoga, learning a new art medium whether it be pottery or throwing darts at balloons filled with paint, oh, and let's not forget therapy. My goal is to create an environment so loving that when my niece comes to visit, she feels safe and deeply loved yet inspired to try new things.

It's to create an environment that even when I feel unstable because of my emotions I know I'm safe and have a place to be free to express myself.

For me my safe place is the beach but since I can't bring the beach to my house I have started to create a safe place in my garden.

My garden consists of butterfly plants called Milkweed and once a year, caterpillars will show up and eat all the leaves, only to turn into cocoons that eventually blossom into the Monarch butterfly. Seeing them flutter around brings me joy, it's so cool to see the transition and it helps put into perspective the hard work that goes into change. You'll also find a few other plants that feed bumblebees and hummingbirds scattered around. My goal is to create a garden that's filled with beautiful creatures and wildlife that bring a sense of peace when in it. My current plant project is a grapevine that will create an arch as you enter the backyard and hopefully, one day, I'll be able to pick the grapes off of it and eat them with my children.

Does growth still scare me? Totally! I feel more prepared in life to take on challenges and hardship than I am to accept growth in a positive direction. Now that I can see that I deserve it to be positive though, I'm opening all these darn doors and windows. Let the growth in and let me introduce myself because I'm finally giving myself permission to evolve and it's terrifyingly exciting.

I also know that the little girl who is me deserves a beautiful future and helping create that is my biggest joy.

The bones of my foundation are built on resilience and courage mixed with kindness and curiosity, and I know my children and future generations will be surrounded by a tremendous amount of love. To me that is the everything. My husband grew up thinking grape vines and vegetable gardens were a normal part of everyone's back yard because of his Papu. What a Greek! I love him! And yes, "my husband", you read that right. Craig and I finally got married and had a wedding. The coolest thing about our marriage is it feels like nothing has changed. We are still best friends, and he has been one of the biggest blessings during my journey. He is patient and kind and helps me work through hard times whether it's by lending an ear or helping me understand a situation from his point of view. Knowing that he will be the father to our children brings me such peace and I know they are in good hands. They will be safe and loved so hard that they'll get annoyed at how loud we are at their sports games or theater productions from the pure excitement to watch them do something they love.

I've known he was good from the way he treated my niece all these years. Sana and I still have a close relationship and she's my world. Whenever she comes over, she is still my focus and I eagerly sit on the couch and ask her to play me a song on her guitar. Maybe I'm biased but she is seriously the coolest and makes me proud and thankful to be a part of her life every day. She is brave and stands up for the voiceless, she has grit, and is compassionate. She isn't afraid to speak her mind and that's something I hope she never lets fade away because watching her grow and take on the world gives me hope for the younger generation. I could talk about her all day and sometimes I do!

When Craig and I first started dating, Sana always wanted to be in the middle of us and was protective of me. As all three of us grew and our lives changed, Craig never stopped showing love for the both of us. Sana would spend weekends at my house and Craig would step to the side and let us do our thing, as Sana got older, she started looking to connect with Craig more and I watched him closely as this happened. They both have a dry sense of humor and like to gang up on me. They share a love for *Harry Potter* on a level I never got to and their conversations are about how the books are better than the movies. As she connects with him, I can tell she is watching the way he treats me and I'm thankful I can show her what a healthy relationship looks and be there for her if she has questions.

One conversation Sana and I had was about jealousy and how we both wished life dealt us better hands at times and this conversation helped me realize a few things.

I have been ridiculously blessed for the people in my life and the wisdom and lessons they have shared with me along the way of a challenging path. Some of those people have things I've never had and honestly never will and that doesn't make me jealous, it shows it's possible. Do I wish I grew up in a beautiful two-parent home believing in dragons and princesses who defeated the evil three-headed dragon through true love, like in the movies? Heck yeah that would be freaking awesome but personally I love my story better, and I wouldn't trade it. It's filled with monsters and darkness too, but the outcome is the princess falling in love with herself, creating a world of magic around her, and inviting those she loves into it. To tell you the truth, I think that story is pretty fantastic.

Am I saying I wasn't jealous at one point of my healing journey? Nope. Trust me it was there and honestly, I was surprised. I was jealous because I wanted it to be easy for me to be loved and for me to have opportunities as easily as some, which is understandable honestly. But the truth is jealousy is ugly and requires too much energy. I had to start looking at my jealous thoughts another way and to remind my brain to have a positive outlook for my life. I realized that the incredible friends I had surrounded myself with at one point of our journey caused me to ask why couldn't I be loved as easily as them and why is it so easy to cheer them on but not myself. My past had slowed me down once again and that made me super jealous.

Once I figured out where that jealous thought was coming from,

I started befriending it and telling it this story: we were all given a foundation to build on. Although others were given the tools and the blueprint to build, I still had the clay, water, my hands and a beautiful rough sketch. A sketch that showed the possibilities! Yes, the person with the blueprint and tools will have an easier time building from their foundation but that doesn't mean they aren't still putting in the work. One thing I yelled into my mind was the amount of work I had put into building myself up. The late hours and tears that came with developing my business, for example, was a struggle that anyone who took a chance in life felt and although they might not be going through the same internal battles as I was, they were still striving to build something. I respected that and loved being their cheerleader. Yeah, they had the blueprint, and I had the sketch, but that meant I had someone to look up to while creating my blueprint for myself. So what if they were building faster than me. If I continue to compare myself and remain jealous the water in my foundation will eventually evaporate and the clay will dry. Instead, I told those thoughts to look at what the Lord has presented us with once again and this was our chance to take that rough sketch and build a solid foundation made with love, with my own hands. Yes, it is going to take longer for me, but my future children will have a blueprint because of me and the love and support of those I surround myself with during the building process, even those with the blueprint or bones already up. Their love never stopped even throughout my healing journey, if anything it became stronger and that's not something to be jealous of. It's something to be thankful for.

It's an interesting approach to jealousy I know, and for now it's working but as I continue to work on the sadness and accept the anger from my past it might need a little editing and that's okay. Being forced to open the box of grief and pain was one of the best things I could have done because without that I would still be living a joyful life of growth but slowly screaming inside. The thoughts and feeling that came from grief, pain, and death provided a life changing perspective.

Queue annoying eye roll but also a side smirk because it's true.

I discovered that the anger that used to scare me is one of my favorite parts of myself now because it was protecting me. I was angry at the abuse that happened to me and Robert and the little girl inside me deserved to scream and to beat the shit out of those blankets with a hockey stick. I know that sadness leads to happiness in a weird crazy way that doesn't always make sense. I know that grief sucks but if it didn't that would mean we wouldn't love as hard as we do and even though some days maybe harder than others it's okay to step back and give yourself the safe place to feel. Just don't forget to give yourself grace. Don't beat yourself up for needing a moment. Beat a pile of sheets with a hockey stick. If you don't have a hockey stick, find a way that works for you to release your anger… just don't murder someone.

Seriously though, find the reasons for those thoughts and then love them so hard that they realize you deserve so much more, that the life you want for yourself is possible. It will take lots of tears, lots of breakdowns, lots of late-night dancing in the garage, and lots of open conversations with yourself, loved ones and a good therapist. It might even call for gel pen flowers and paint brushes.

Whatever you do though, don't hold it in and don't push it down. There is so much beauty in this world that you deserve to be a part of. I don't know exactly what you've gone through, but I can say I'm sorry that you have been hurt and are hurting. Our stories may not be the same, but the truth is, pain is painful and it fucking sucks. The monsters who hurt us are just that – monsters – and monsters don't deserve to win. They don't get to take your happiness and pride away because they are weak and hurt children. As beautiful as this world is, it is also filled with darkness and that darkness will try so hard to take your shine. Fuck the darkness and those weak people who have nothing better to do but hurt you. Their lives are sad and they see something in you that makes them want to hurt you and bring you down. Don't give them that power.

You deserve a beautiful life and although it wasn't dealt the way you wished it was, that doesn't mean you don't deserve happiness. It will just take a bit more for you to get there, and trust me it's annoying, but wouldn't you rather be annoyed while working on building yourself up again than angry and not moving forward in a way that will help you get what you want out of life?

Trust me, good things are worth the work and when you receive the reward it's so much sweeter.

And do you know what? It's beautiful! You're beautiful!

And filled with magic

And stardust.

And tiny angry emotions that need to be loved.

So, love them and know you are worthy of great things. Also know that life is going to get hard at times, but it's only a season and the storm will pass. The first time you encounter those moments may create fear, but I hope you give your emotions a safe place to be heard and go in feeling courageous. Look fear in the eye and say you can't stop me. That will be even scarier but doing it even while you're afraid is better than letting the fear win. The only thing that you should let win is yourself and the chance at having a beautiful life.

Thank you for reading my story. I wrote this book during a time when I needed another way to try to understand what was happening to me. I remembered writing the poem I gave to my mom and how I was finally able to say what I felt. Something in me called me back to putting pen to paper and this book has given me that power back. I may not always have the right words, and plenty of times those words are chaotic, with random thoughts all coming out at once, but that's what rewrites are for, am I right?

The truth is, as I close this book, I feel like it is okay to move forward now and, while I am still working with my therapist on missing the ball of trauma, I am not looking to hold it as much as I did before. I see it now and smile as I place it in the box and shut the door. I feel peace knowing it won't hurt me again, no matter how beautiful I made it seem.

Writing might not be everyone's method, but for me it has helped, and I encourage you, my little readers, to write. The words don't have to make sense and they don't have to be pretty. Let them flow and let what comes to mind out on the page. It doesn't have to make sense to others and you don't even have to show it to anyone; do it for yourself. Because that little person inside you who was hurt deserves to share their voice and they deserve love and don't forget that that little person is you and that you also deserve love and to have the chance to build your foundation for yourself and for your future generations.

Now get outta here and go blossom, cause a ruckus in the world, and if you're feeling it, go for a run in the rain.

ACKNOWLEDGMENTS

HI MOM
WAVES
I WROTE A BOOK! CRAZY, I KNOW! HEAVEN DOESN'T HAVE AN ADDRESS, SO YOUR SPIRIT MUST COME HERE AND HAUNT A LIBRARY. ENJOY! AND THANK YOU FOR ALWAYS BELIEVING IN ME AND HELPING ME SEE MY LIGHT, ESPECIALLY WHEN I COULDN'T SEE IT MYSELF.

TO MY HUSBAND,
HEY THERE, GOOD LOOKIN'!
SEXY AWKWARD WINK
THANK YOU FOR THE ENDLESS LOVE AND NEVER-ENDING SUPPORT DURING MY WRITING JOURNEY. FOR THE REMINDERS TO DRINK WATER, EAT FOOD, AND, MOST IMPORTANTLY, YOUR PRESENCE AND KNOWING WHEN I NEEDED TO TAKE A MENTAL BREAK AND REST. IF IT WEREN'T FOR YOU, I'D BE STARVING OVER A DYING COMPUTER WITH A PUFFY FACE AND DRIED TEARS.

HAVING YOU AS A PART OF THIS CRAZY ADVENTURE WAS A BLESSING, AND I'M GENUINELY THANKFUL FOR YOU; AND YOUR FANTASTIC BUTT. KEEP ROCKING, HANDSOME, AND THANKS FOR BEING MY BEST FRIEND.

TO MY NIECE AND DAUGHTER
HUGS
YOU TWO HAVE GIVEN ME THE GIFT OF KNOWING UNCONDITIONAL LOVE, AND I CAN NEVER THANK YOU ENOUGH FOR THAT. PLEASE KNOW YOU ARE MAGIC AND LOVED MORE THAN EVERY STAR IN THE UNIVERSE. BUT, MOST IMPORTANTLY, KNOW YOU ARE WORTHY OF GREAT THINGS, AND NO ONE CAN TAKE YOUR SHINE WITHOUT YOUR PERMISSION.

NOW GO OUT THERE AND DO GREAT THINGS BUT PLEASE STAY SAFE AND HYDRATED!

TO MY READERS AND FRIENDS
HIGH FIVE THROUGH THE PAPER
THANK YOU FOR BELIEVING IN ME AND FOR ENDLESS LOVE AND SUPPORT OVER THE YEARS! THANK YOU TO THOSE WHO VOLUNTEERED TO READ MY MANUSCRIPT DRAFTS AND MEET FOR COFFEE A BILLION TIMES. TO THOSE WHO WERE THERE IN MY TIME OF UNCERTAINTY AND QUESTIONING IF I SHOULD CONTINUE THIS BOOK, I WALKED AWAY FEELING LIGHTER FROM EVERY CONVERSATION. I CAN'T THANK YOU ENOUGH FOR BEING A FRIEND DURING A MASSIVE TRANSITION IN MY LIFE.

TO NERO
BELLY RUBS
I KNOW YOU CAN'T READ, BUT OUR DAILY WALKS, WHETHER THROUGH THE PARK OR ON A NATURE HIKE, HELPED GROUND ME, AND YOU'RE THE MOST HANDSOME BEST BOY THERE EVER WAS.

www.ingramcontent.com/pod-product-compliance
Lightning Source LLC
Chambersburg PA
CBHW072043160426
43197CB00014B/2605